China Diary of a

VENERABLE
FOREIGN
EXPERT

PATRICIA ENDRESS

My history is a drop in the ocean of China's history.

Patricia Thornton

To

Danielle and Elizabeth for putting up
with their peripatetic mother

and to

Qiong Zhang, Yang Yan, Xu Ping and Gu Yun
for making China my second home

In the water city of ZhouZhuang, the boatman offered the author a chance to pole the boat.

CONTENTS

Changzhou 2008   223

Afterword   257

INTRODUCTION

China Notes is a collection of accounts of my years in China. On and off from 2000 to 2008, I taught in a small college in Changzhou, China, a city midway between Shanghai and Nanjing and one of the new enterprise zones. During that time, I saw a drab city become a modern and lovely place complete with a Walmart, Kentucky Fried Chicken, McDonald's, Pizza Hut, and Starbucks. A dinosaur theme park and a pagoda drew countless tourists and the city swarmed with foreigners. The "small college" where I taught morphed into a university.

My accounts of my life during this time were sent to *The Sherman Sentinel*, a newspaper in my hometown of Sherman, Connecticut. They describe my day-to-day life, the students and fellow teachers I met, new foods I ate, changes in the city and school, and sometimes history and cultural background. I found my position in Changzhou through the Council on International Education Exchanges. The Council also provided a week of information about teaching in China, some language lessons, and tours of Beijing's famous attractions, among them the Great Wall, the Forbidden City, and the Summer Palace. I remember the cost of this was around a thousand dollars plus airfare. That summer before I left, I also took a course on Chinese Cultural History. My teacher, Dr. Qiong Zhang, was a recent graduate of Harvard and also became a friend. I picked up a few Chinese language books for some basic words and concepts and read many of the recently translated books out of China. All this helped. As it turned out, I was the oldest person of 126 would-be teachers the Council hosted that year. I was a retired professor from a New Jersey community college and soon found I was afforded a special place at dinners and official gatherings. I also learned I was now a foreign expert, and because my age made me so often venerated, I dubbed myself Venerable Foreign Expert. The notes I sent home were all signed as the Venerable Foreign Expert; they have been eliminated here as being unnecessarily repetitious. The notes are not great literature, and the reader will find some repetition, often necessary for the reader picking up a *Sentinel* for the first time.

A postscript: My little town of Sherman has fewer than four thousand people, many of them summer people. Yet three of us have taught in China: Jonathan Fazzone, Taylor Loeb, and me. Taylor is currently teaching in Changzhou University, once my little college and now a "daxue."

CHANGZHOU
2000–2001

OFF TO TEACH IN CHINA

As many of my Sherman friends and neighbors know, I am headed for China for a year's teaching stint. My berth is the Jiangsu Institute of Petrochemical Technology, a school founded approximately twenty-five years ago and, as the name indicates, houses a predominantly engineering college. The city of Changzhou, where the school is located, lies about two hours west of Shanghai and an hour and a half east of Nanjing, just south of the Yangzi in the Jiangsu province. The Chinese government has declared Changzhou an Industrial Development Area, so the population that now stands at 3.6 million—small as Chinese cities go—is growing. The Institute itself accounts for three thousand regular students and about twelve hundred adult students.

The campus includes twenty-eight hectares—or almost seventy acres—and all the foreign teachers live on campus. I shall have a bed/sitting room with my own bath but shall share the kitchen. This gives all us foreigners—many from Europe, and many from Australia and New Zealand—an added intercultural experience. I am told that at least one other American has been placed at the Institute and another teacher is from England. My teaching includes two courses of English conversation for first-year English majors and two courses of business writing for the third-year business majors. The English major is new to the school, and I expect to do a lot of sharing with the faculty there. My position pays a salary of 2,200 RMB, or about $300 a month, considered a princely sum in China. I also am to receive a travel allowance of about $125 a semester. Keep these figures in mind, as I'm told the Chinese have a habit of changing the terms of a contract, and I may be in for some surprises.

My "waiban," or foreign leader, who is in charge of us "waiguoren" (foreigners), has already sent me a welcoming letter. She is Professor Yang Yan, and you will probably be hearing more about her. The waiban at Chinese schools and colleges can be a helpful angel or can make life hell. I am delighted that Yang Yan comes with a good reputation from foreign teachers, and her emails have been warm and helpful.

You may be interested to know that America is known in pinyin (the alphabetized version of the Chinese characters) as "meiguo," or beautiful country, and I am a "meiguoren," or a beautiful country person. How can I help but love a people who confirm what I have always felt about myself.

My year in China will begin with a week's orientation and sightseeing in Beijing. Of course, that includes the Great Wall, the Forbidden City, and all the other high spots. Then it's on to Changzhou, where the real adventure begins. I expect to see Jonathan Fazzone, now studying in Shanghai. He has kindly offered to show me the ropes in that city—and has even promised to take me to some of the restaurants that feature rat on the menu. Only kidding, he said. I'll see. One of my colleagues has told me that in China, if it moves, they eat it. I've decided not to ask what I'm eating and pray I won't be told. All this, and chopsticks too.

BEIJING

After a day's flight, I am finally in Beijing and a hotel for a week's orientation, Chinese lessons, touring, and banquets. There are about 126 of us foreign teachers, one of the smaller Council groups to teach in China this year. There is a large contingent of Australians and New Zealanders, many of them well-traveled. About twenty-six of us are Americans, many of whom I met on the flight here. Among them, I particularly enjoyed Brian, a lawyer on sabbatical, and Erin, one of my email correspondents. I also met Nell, an intelligent young woman with whom I walked during our free time. She, Brian, and I shall be teaching at colleges, whereas the other Americans in the group shall be teaching in primary and secondary schools. I discovered that I am the oldest member of the group; the youngest are only twenty. I also learned that my age entitled me to be seated with all the officials at the head table. I would have appreciated this more had I had some practice with chopsticks.

The next day, the group received instructions on what was expected of us as foreigners in China. First, the head of Council in China told us to remember we were guests in China and, second, that our lives would be lived in a fishbowl, followed by some instructions about our behavior. Later that day, we were introduced to Mr. Wu of the Security Administration for Foreign Expert Affairs. Every teacher who comes to China is under the jurisdiction of SAFEA. The officials refer to the foreign teachers as foreign experts. Mr. Wu was one of the officials of the Beijing foreign affairs office, the central office, and we learned that every city, province, school, college, and university has its own SAFEA office. He told us what to avoid: politics and religion and any subject that proselytized a particular political system or agenda and a religion. Later that day, we heard from several of the groups who had been teaching in China and they were most informative about the students, curfews, and differences between large and small towns. One young man said to think of being in a kayak without an oar and having to learn how to find and use an oar to help avoid rapids and whirlpools.

That evening, SAFEA hosted a banquet, and my gray head earned me a seat at the head table. There were several speeches in both English and Chinese. Later, Nell reminded me that when Mr. Wu spoke, he said not that the children of China were the future of China but that they were the future of the world. There's something to ponder.

LESSONS AND SIGHTSEEING

We are being immersed in Chinese. Our teacher, Yan (a popular girl's name in China), is a student at Beijing University, as are all of our Chinese teachers, who work part-time for the Council. They are really delightful, and I enjoy talking with them. As for us, a group of Americans, Brits, Scots and Irish, we are a sorry bunch. Still, we seem to be picking up some Chinese. After lunch, we visited Tiananmen Square and the Forbidden City. The Square is enormous and the Forbidden City magnificent. Because the Chinese believe in the harmony of yin and yang, of balance, every building is exactly duplicated off the center of the main buildings that make up the heart of the city. There were more places than I can remember, so my overall impression is that of red walls, golden roof-tops, dragons and phoenix, blue and green tiles, earth, wood, and metal. The carving must have taken years to create; even the roofs with their wonderful curves that turn up at the ends had carvings on them. Roof ends turn up in order to turn away any bad spirits and return them to wherever they had come from. I liked the bronze lions and dragons, the huge bronze pots, and the dragonhead rain spouts. As for the colors, if I remember correctly, the blue and green tiles were the colors that signify the Ming dynasty, just as black is the color of the Qin dynasty (if you saw the Chinese film *Hero*, which takes place in the Qin dynasty, black predominates). In many Chinese films, the colors are often a clue to the dynasty, and therefore the time period. Yellow belongs to the emperors.

The gardens surrounding the area are also lovely and, for me, an especially nice place to relax. The weather here in Beijing is hot and sticky this time of year.

INTERNET CAFÉS

Chinese cities, both large and small, have internet cafés where one can email or play games. Beijing is no exception, and we located one a short walk from our hotel. It was pricey and crowded, and we had to wait for a computer to be freed up before we could email. The café was also smoke-filled as so many Chinese men and boys smoke. Cigarette smoke doesn't help the already polluted air of Beijing. Coal-powered industries, the encroaching desert, car and bus fumes create a permanent haze over the city, some days so bad the city often limits motor-driven traffic. We often wondered if Beijing residents ever saw the stars or moon.

There is constant construction here. A new walk is being built a few blocks from our hotel, all by hand and all with tile. The ground is leveled by hand tools; work here seems to be done in very labor-intensive ways. I also saw women sweeping the walks with brooms made of bound twigs, the kind one sees in fairy tales with witches' brooms. The women wore surgical masks to keep them from breathing the dust, and there was plenty of dust I experienced walking by where the street and sidewalk had just been swept.

Bicycles are everywhere; I haven't seen so many bicycles since Amsterdam. A large part of Beijing's population still travels by bike. Some of them have carts attached to the rear and carry everything from tiles and laundry to produce and meat. All of this competes with cars, taxis, and buses. There are, as I suspected, many accidents and a large number of cyclists are killed each year. I wouldn't dare ride a bike in a major Chinese city. As for a smaller one, I'll see when I get there.

THE GREAT WALL

A visit to the Great Wall is obligatory for a visitor to China. All the tourist pictures I have ever seen of the Great Wall show people strolling along a level expanse. The truth is that most of the Great Wall is steps, countless steps. What makes the climb more difficult is the varying level of the steps. Several are one-brick high, varied by another one or two that are two bricks high, and then a whopper of a three-brick-high step. This makes finding a pace difficult. Nor does it help to climb in the polluted atmosphere of Beijing. There are countless stories about the Great Wall, a large segment of which was built by China's first emperor, Qin Shi Huangdi, who among other things unified China and was responsible for the army of terra cotta soldiers in Xi'an. Qin Shi Huangdi was also known for his cruelty and one of those imperial cruelties was the impressment of millions of young men to build the wall. One story has it that the mortar is made of the crushed skeletons of the many workers who died there. My favorite story, however, is of the young couple, recently married and deeply in love, who were separated when the husband was impressed into service building the wall. A year passed and the young wife heard nothing. When another year passed, she went to the wall. She learned her husband had died. The tears she wept were so copious that a large segment of the wall dissolved and washed away.

Other Beijing musts are the Forbidden City and the Summer Palace. I preferred the latter, which is set along a large lake with countless pavilions, walkways, sculptures, and gardens. Tourists, who include many Chinese as well as foreigners, can take a dragon boat trip on the lake. I wondered when I walked through all this how Louis XIV would have felt, since he considered Versailles the most magnificent building in existence. The Summer Palace would have outclassed him. Although the pillars in many ancient Chinese buildings look as if they are made of stone, they are actually made of wood and heavily lacquered. This construction burns easily, so many of the buildings the tourist sees are not originals but replacements.

Pagodas dot most Chinese hills. These are Buddhist structures. Unlike many of the Buddhist monasteries and other religious buildings destroyed during the Cultural Revolution, the pagodas remain—most likely too big to bother destroying. The pagoda in Yangzhou stands eight stories high—eight being a significant number in Buddhist philosophy. On each floor of this pagoda are varying statues of Buddha showing varying aspects of his character. And on each floor, there were four similar statues of the Buddha, each facing in a different direction. A large gilded Buddha was one of four on one floor, and a wonderful white jade Buddha was one of four on another floor. Religion has made a big comeback in China, and Christian churches as well as Buddhist and Daoist temples are again frequented. The thought is that as people have lost faith in the certainties of early Communism, they seek such certainty in religion. Although the official religion of the government is atheism, I have heard that even Communist Party officials are known to visit Buddhist temples—I like the idea of closet Buddhists.

CHINESE TOILETS

Most toilets in China are squats, that is, a hole or a "chunnel" over which you squat to relieve yourself. For many years, squats were also common in Europe; in Europe, torn squares of newspaper served as toilet paper. In China, it's best to have a small package of tissues always with you, for there is no paper of any kind available. Although most of us think chunnel refers to the tunnel between England and Europe, in China it refers to a long-tiled depression for use by several people. Some have private cubicles; others, none. At any rate, if you must use a chunnel, it's best to be at the top of the incline, where the system flushes, rather than at the bottom, where the system empties out.

All this being said, your Chinese visit will sometimes include the toilet you're used to at home. Shanghai museums and hotels have lovely Western toilets, and for the elderly whose knees would prevent them from rising, some bus and railroad stations include a Western toilet. Also, in the traditional six-story apartment complexes, the first floor is generally occupied by elders, and these apartments have Western toilets.

When a group of us go out to a teahouse or restaurant, we hope the toilet will be a sit-down. Usually, the first person whose bladder can no longer hold it comes back with the word: regular or squat. At the airport, one fellow came back to tell us the toilets were squat, but the walls and floors were lovely black marble. This prompted another person to pronounce it a royal squat.

This is simply one if the adjustments you will have to make if you travel to China. You may comfort yourself with the knowledge that squats are actually better for you and a healthier way to go to the bathroom.

INTRODUCTION TO CHINESE CUISINE

Our week in Beijing also included some wonderful banquets. The first was our welcoming dinner by the Security Administration for Foreign Expert Affairs. A Chinese banquet is a feast for both the eyes and the palate. To begin, a number of small appetizers are placed on what may be deemed a giant Lazy Susan. These dishes consist of small slices of meat, slivers of vegetables, such as zucchini, perhaps a spicy cabbage, something sweet, and so on. To eat something, I simply spin to the dish I want and take a bit onto my plate with my chopsticks. I am now pretty good at this and, yesterday, to my delight, actually got a peanut onto my plate and into my mouth without dropping it. Most of us feel we could make a meal of the appetizers. but they are only the beginning of countless meat and vegetable dishes that appear one after the other. The meal generally finishes with a sweet or fruit, and the fruit most commonly eaten here is watermelon.

A warning about eating in China: don't finish everything on your plate, because you will be given more. Here, the Chinese figure if you have cleaned your plate, you must still be hungry. This goes for wine and beer as well, and at our first banquet, I went home with a slight buzz.

There were two other banquets. Beijing is famous for its Peking duck. This is no ordinary duck, but one that comes from a particular area in China, is force-fed, and done in on the forty-fifth day of its life, all to be served up in varying forms at a banquet. The duck is well-used, something akin to the old line that the only thing on a pig that isn't used is its squeal. One hundred separate slices can be carved from a Peking duck. The restaurant where we ate also hosted President George H. W. Bush and is also where he threw up. That did not happen to any of us, and the food was exceptional.

Our last banquet came on a Saturday evening, a good-bye feast at a Thai restaurant. The food here was a bit spicier than most of what we ate at other banquets, and the rice was steamed in bamboo. I enjoyed the spicy cabbage and the curry soup in particular, and throughout the meal, Thai dancers in traditional dress performed several ethnic dances for us. A lovely way to say farewell to Beijing.

I would like to add that I have command of many Chinese words and sentences but, like most of us, am struggling with the language. Still, in this time, I have earned my title of Venerable Foreign Expert.

CHANGZHOU AT LAST

We are a big group being flown to Changzhou, where we are to teach, and the coolness of the airplane after the sweltering heat of Beijing is a welcome relief. The relief lasts only an hour. We step from the plane into what feels like a sauna, and we are met by a group of officials from the college. From the time I heard from Yang Yan at JSIPT, I could not come up with an image of her, so the small pretty woman in a classical silk Chinese dress, looking a little wilted from the heat, was not exactly a surprise but a welcome picture. She was accompanied by Mr. Zhou, her boss and the SAFEA department head, and several college vice presidents.

We are taken to the college guesthouse, where we are placed in our rooms and shown the kitchen, the laundry room and the office. This last is a small room with a TV, a couch, and a computer. Our rooms themselves are large, about hotel size, and hold a full-sized bed, desk, armoire, TV, chairs, and small end tables. The en suite bathroom features a toilet, sink, and tub with a hot-water tank that runs as it heats. The room is fairly clean, the bathroom filthy. I loved being finally able to unpack and store my things and, after cleaning the bathroom, showered and slept well. The next night, the college president and others from the college will be hosting us at a banquet. The "us" are two English girls, Alex and Anushka, and a lovely young Canadian, Leona. I make up the fourth. Leona has been at the college for two weeks and knows her way around the town, stores, and restaurants. She has established a solid relationship with Yang Yan, our waiban.

At our banquet, I learned an interesting aspect of Chinese "equality." The driver of the group also had a place at the dinner table. He was the one who belched at the end of the meal. I also learned that the red peppers in one of the chicken dishes was hot enough to make smoke come out of my ears. Instead, however, it brought tears to my eyes as the rest of my face turned crimson. I had always thought the red paper flakes I enjoy on my pizza slices were as hot as it can get. I learned better that evening.

SETTLING IN—SORT OF

Today, we signed our contracts and received our first pay. This will shortly disappear, as we are planning a trip to Xi'an for the National Day holiday—celebrating October 1, 1949, when the Communist Party took over the country. There will be sixteen of us going, and I shall see Nell again, as she will be one of the group. Along with my pay, I received my schedule at long last. I will teach writing to the business administration class, an English conversation class of young faculty, and after the holiday, a conversation class for the students in the tourism program. I am also responsible for several schoolwide lectures and have no idea what they will cover.

Later that day, I was offered a job editing copy for a new dinosaur park to be built in the city. The officials wanted an experienced editor to proof the copy that was to be displayed on the walls. The only problem was that significant changes were not possible, just minor ones. I declined, as it was apparent that I couldn't okay something that possibly had real problems, and I could see myself getting into a real hassle. Yang Yan added to what I felt, telling me that the information had already been put up on the walls and they wanted an "English expert" to okay it. This way, if anything wrong was discovered, they could say an English expert had okayed it. Yang Yan agreed it was best for me not to be involved.

An email from one of my former colleagues wrote that registration had been "crazy." I replied that she didn't know what craziness was. Not only has my schedule been changed but the days, starting times for the courses, and room numbers haven't been assigned.

For instance, the business-writing course was to have begun on August 26th, the day before I arrived in China. The young faculty I am to teach will meet on Wednesday, but I have no room number; the conversation class for the tourism students will begin after the national holiday, and I am not sure what else I am to teach, except that I am to offer lectures on business-writing for the general student body. I can schedule these myself just so long as I give a two-week notice in advance so students can be notified. I shall have a few other lecture and English club responsibilities as well. So far, I have one class roster with twenty-three students. Meanwhile, I have a lunch date on Tuesday with Professor Xu, a nice woman, but her English is difficult to understand, and she does eat a lot of garlic.

MY CHINESE NAME AND MY NEW HOME

Just before I left Beijing for my teaching post in Changzhou, my Chinese language teacher gave me my Chinese name. It is An Cui Sha, pronounced "An Tswee Sha." An is my last name, and Cui Sha is my first name, and if pronounced quickly, it sounds something like Tricia. My name is made up of characters, chosen for their meaning, and my characters read "tranquil," "fresh," and "highly paid." The fresh really means creative, not sassy, and highly paid is what I am by Chinese standards. This is probably the first time I have earned more than a college president, and it feels very right somehow. My Chinese name is required for all my work papers and other documents, and I am learning to write the characters. My attempts look like a first grader's attempt at printing her name. Very embarrassing.

My new home also presents some new challenges. Cities in China have their own special aromas. In Beijing, the city smelled of coal dust and dirt. There's a story about a foreigner who jogged in Beijing, and when she went home was told by her physician that her lungs were the same as if she had smoked five packs of cigarettes a day. As for Changzhou, when the wind blows a certain way, the city has the combined smell of a Manhattan subway urinal and the New Milford Nestlé plant. Happily, this odor isn't constant.

On our first day here, we four foreign teachers were treated to a banquet in Changzhou's best restaurant. Chinese banquets are magnificent, so it pays to learn how to use chopsticks. I have improved considerably since I arrived here. I would boast about my ability to pick up a peanut at a time with my chopsticks except that there are certain jellied items and dumplings that managed to skitter across my plate and sometimes across the table as well. The four of us happily noted that our Chinese friends sometimes had the same trouble.

As for what I eat, that varies from day to day. I have developed a liking for duck's blood soup, which tastes a bit like tofu, except it's blood, and is served in a hot and sour broth. As for the more exotic foods—dog, cat, snake, and mice—I pass. Mr. Zhou, the head of foreign affairs, eats all of the above. His favorite, however, is mice, not, he told us, big ones, but those little ones that come into our homes for warmth when the frost hits. Leona asked him if he ate them cooked or if he ate "sushi" mice. I'm happy to tell you that he eats them cooked.

Not everyone eats the above exotic foods; our waiban, Professor Yang Yan, eats none of them. Still, I have seen only one dog since I have arrived in China, and that was far too scrawny to make a meal. I keep thinking of all the dogs in Paris and wonder what the Chinese would think about this.

A HOLIDAY AND WE'VE HARDLY WORKED

On October 1, National Day, which celebrates the successful Communist takeover of China in 1949, we have our first big holiday, and so, we are taking a group trip to Xi'an, the ancient capital of China, established by Qin Shi Huangdi, the first emperor and the first to unify China. But more about this later.

Today was the Moon Festival, and like many of the festivals in China, there is a story behind it. My students supplied it for me. There were once two suns that dried up everything. HouYi, the great archer, shot the two suns with his magic arrow. (The one sun, I interpret as becoming the moon.) In revenge, HouYi's wife was taken up into the sky where she became the lady in the moon. She is very beautiful, fills the eyes, but can never be reached. One can gaze at the moon and see her there with her pet rabbit and frog. On moon day, families get together and eat delicious foods and moon cakes while gazing at the moon. Yang Yan presented us foreign experts with a beautiful red tin with a raised gold dragon and phoenix on its top and moon cakes inside. These taste a bit like fruitcake and are very filling as well as delicious.

There are other significant festivals. As one of the Chinese teachers told me, "We Chinese like holidays." The most famous holiday of all is Spring Festival. It is a lunar holiday and is particularly long. This year, the break for the school is six weeks. This allows families who live a long distance away travel time. The holiday itself is a combination of our Thanksgiving and Christmas. The food is both special and plentiful; the children receive presents, clothes, and sometimes toys and money. Of all the special events in China, this is the one my students talk about most.

Another holiday that I found most interesting is often referred to as the Dragon Boat Festival. It's celebrated on May 5th in the lunar calendar. "This day, people eat *zongzi*, a kind of food made of glutinous rice dumplings wrapped in bamboo leaves," explained my student Xu Shuling. In some places, people also have dragon boat competitions. The festival commemorates the great Chinese poet Qu Yuan. He was a courtier in the Kingdom of Chu during the Warring States period (940–278 BCE). He advised the king against forming an alliance with Qin, who was to conquer all the various kingdoms and unify China. Qu's rivals in the court convinced the king he was being falsely advised, and Qu was exiled. When Qin conquered Chu as he had predicted, Qu Yuan drowned himself in the river as a protest against a tyrannical emperor. "Because the people didn't want the fish to eat his body, they cooked many, many zongzi to feed the fish," Xu Shuling said. "Today, people still eat zongzi, but just as a happy feast."

BICYCLES AND A TEMPLE

Anyone who thinks there is no individualism in Communist countries has yet to travel on a Chinese road. There are, first of all, the bicycles, the chief mode of transportation in China. They are everywhere—bicycles with single riders, bicycles with passengers, bicycles with carts carrying everything from trash and laundry to tiles and meat. (The meat flapping in the dust of the roads is enough to make one convert to vegetarianism on the spot.) Then come the motor scooters, these, too, with one or more passengers. There are not many cars in Changzhou, but there are enough taxis and buses to create considerable motor vehicle traffic. Drivers and cyclists go wherever there is a space, whether on the right side of the road or not or whatever the color of the stoplights. Riding in a taxi or bus holds more thrills than the world's fastest, highest roller coaster. Crossing the street is my most dangerous activity in China. I am getting good at it, however.

This past weekend, a group of us visited a Daoist monastery on the outskirts of Changzhou. Like many monasteries, it sits on top of a mountain and is reached by stairs. According to one of our group, there is one monastery that takes more than two hours to reach by stairs. Those who make it are guaranteed to live a hundred years. Our temple took only an hour of stairs, so I figure I'm good until I'm eighty-five.

Getting to the temple was supposed to be a two-bus ride; however, our student guide made a deal with our bus driver to take us all the way and, for an added two yuan a piece, also wait for us and take us home. It was a deal. I found myself wondering as we rode home about the people who may have been waiting for the bus. Wasn't there a schedule? And what about passengers?

My Chinese progresses slowly. I ask my students to give me a new word at the end of every class, and, of course, to get food, I must learn many words. There are several expressions I particularly enjoy. For instance, I answer the phone with "wei" (pronounced "way"); say "hao ba" ("how bah") for "okay"; greet people with "ni hao" ("nee how"); and say "zaitian" ("dsi tee en") for "goodbye." But my favorite expression is "mama huhu" ("mama hoo hoo"). Literally, the expression translates as "tiger horse," but it means "so-so." When I used this in class, my students all giggled as they do whenever I use a Chinese expression. Partly, they are also laughing at my pronunciation.

We foreigners are something of a celebrity here. Changzhou is a small city, as cities go in China, so foreigners are something of an oddity. We have seen several motor scooter drivers and cyclists nearly go off the road they are so busy looking us over. One evening when the four of us foreign teachers were at a restaurant, the entire waitstaff surrounded our table to check us out. Of the four of us, I am the oldest. In fact, I believe I am the oldest teacher on campus, and this means everyone on campus from the president on down defers to me. I'm not sure I always enjoy this, as I sometimes think everyone on campus expects me to drop dead at any moment.

This next week, a group of us will visit Xi'an during the national holiday. I shall have more to write about then. Also, I plan to tell you about the eating habits we foreigners have all picked up along with our chopsticks.

THE YOUNG FACULTY CLASS

Today, I had to interview twenty college faculty members for the young faculty English class. Adding English to their academic profiles would raise their salaries, true also for becoming proficient in Japanese or Korean, the countries China most trades with. They were all such lovely people, although not exactly "young" (most likely relatively new hires). Many of them were women and most of them with pretty decent English. They were shy about speaking, refused a compliment—"Oh no, my English is very poor"— ducked their heads, put their hands over their mouths, and giggled. Of the twenty-one who came to be interviewed, Miss Zhou and Yang Yan and I decided sixteen were ready for the class. There were two problems. Miss Zhou told me that the man with the very poor English was a big man on campus and powerful in the hierarchy. So I said, "Why, of course, he is in the class." She and Yang Yan laughed. The other problem was Liu Hong who was way ahead of the other students, and I felt would be bored in the class. Miss Zhou suggested he be made class monitor who could help me and his classmates as well. I thought it a wonderful solution and also how wonderful Miss Zhou and YangYan were at finding face-saving solutions to awkward situations.

I later learned how difficult those interviews were for the applicants. In a note at the end of the term, Na Hai Bo wrote, "I remember the first time I met you. It was the first time I faced a foreign person, and I was too nervous to understand you."

I also learned why Liu Hong was so able in English. He had passed the CET-6 test in English, which is quite a feat. Students told me that a student had to know at least 50,000 English words in order to pass. I am not certain I know 50,000 English words. Consider, for instance, that the Bible is said to be limited to a vocabulary of 7000 words.

Also, over the semester, Liu Hong shared many Chinese stories with me and added a lot to my class as well. The young faculty became one of my favorite classes.

AN OFFICIAL WELCOMING DINNER

Just before the group of foreign teachers left for Xi'an, the Changzhou city officials invited all the foreign teachers as well as heads of new businesses being started here to a banquet celebrating the fifty-first anniversary of the People's Republic of China. The founding date is known as National Day and falls on October 1.

As the oldest foreign teacher here, I sat at the head table, where the service was extra special. I sat opposite the mayor of Changzhou and between the deputy mayor and the local supervisor of Foreign Expert Affairs. Although there were several foreign businessmen at the table, I was closer to a nice young man from Sweden, and I remember him in particular, as we were both hoping that our chopsticks didn't make fools of us. We did quite well. Among the dishes we ate were a snail-and-mushroom pie covered with an excellent puff pastry and turtle soup. I'm not sure I ate any turtle meat, and if I did, turtle meat tastes surprisingly like duck. I mention my version of turtle soup because another foreign teacher who was given that dish in her town said there was a whole turtle at the bottom of her soup. To eat it, she had to remove the shell and dig in. She was still new to using chopsticks so unluckily dropped a bit of a dish into her wine glass. The wine was for a toast in honor of the new teachers, and her hosts didn't know what to do. If they drank, she would be embarrassed, and if they didn't drink, there would be no toast. I'm not quite sure how this situation resolved itself, but since she came to Xi'an with our group here, I expect some face-saving solution was found. (As it turned out, everyone at the table dropped a bit of food in his or her wine glass.)

Eating habits change here, and I'm afraid by the time all of us come home from our stay in China, our families will have to keep us in solitary for a week to retrain our manners. There is, first of all, the boarding-house reach. If I want something, I just lean across everyone else and grab what I want with my chopsticks. Then, if I eat anything with bones in it, I spit them on the table, as there is no place else for them to go. As for eating noodles, which I do quite frequently, I haven't had as much fun since I was a child and tried sucking up whole strands of spaghetti. Noodles in China are kept extra long, as long noodles are said to give you a long life. There is no way anyone, much less me, can wind all the noodle length around a pair of chopsticks, so slurp, slurp it is. And if we don't wish to have all our food drop on the table, we keep our heads as close as possible to the plates or the bowls. So far, only one of the foreign teachers with me at Jiangsu Institute has finished a meal with a belch.

My time here in the polluted air has has also made me understand why so many Chinese constantly spit. The air has given most of us coughs and upper-respiratory congestion, and there is a constant need to get rid of this. No, I haven't taken up the habit of spitting yet, but that's because one of my students has given me some "pang da hai," traditional Chinese medicine, to help clear my congestion. Pang da hai looks like a small version of a peach pit, all wrinkly and black. It's put in hot water, much as I would to make a cup of tea, and expands into a lovely flower-like gelatinous substance. It tastes fine, and I always feel much better after I drink it.

I have been so celebrated here that I rather expect a banquet when I return to Sherman, but only after my manners have been restored.

XI'AN AT LAST

Xi'an, China's ancient capital, has a population of six million, making our home city of Changzhou, population 3.6 million, seem a village by comparison. Xi'an is the burial place of Qin Shi Huangdi, China's first emperor and the first to unify China. He is best known to foreigners for the army of terra cotta soldiers buried in his tomb. He is also credited with the building of the Great Wall, although actually he merely extended several of the walls that had been built earlier. Qin Shi Huangdi's more important contributions, however, include the standardization of the characters that make up Chinese writing as well as the standardization of weights, measures, coins, and the size of the axles on carts. He is also known for his cruelty. Thousands of impressed laborers died building the Great Wall and all of the artisans who produced the army of terra cotta soldiers are said to have been killed when their work was finished, so no one would ever discover the secret of how they were made. Qin Shi Huangdi can also go down in history as one of the first book burners.

He didn't trust scholars, and he particularly hated Confucius. He ruled as emperor for a short fifteen years, dying in 210 BCE. His unification of China permitted the flourishing of the Han dynasty that followed and lasted for more than four hundred years. Not only did this dynasty produce some of China's first great poets and artists but it also opened the country to the outside. Xi'an became the end city of the silk road, its silk prized by the Roman patricians.

One of the more interesting places to me was the Xi'an jade factory we visited that morning. Jade is called the Chinese diamond; it has a hardness number of 8.5, compared to diamond's hardness number of ten. Both can cut glass. The harder the jade, the more valuable it is. We saw many lovely bowls, which, when held up to the light, showed varying shades. One seemingly black jade bowl had tints of green when held up to the light; an orange bowl had lovely shades of ivory and yellow.

Upstairs in the factory, we watched the workers polishing the jade, which begins as nothing more than a dusty-looking hunk of stone. From this comes a variety of statues: Buddhas; Yu Yuan, the goddess of mercy; animals and birds. Each worker is also an artist, and the designs are unique to him or her. One woman was finishing an elaborate peacock of black jade, and if I could have afforded it, I would have happily shown it off to you in Sherman. I settled for a "chop." This is a seal, or stamp, and it is often seen on Chinese works of art and bears the artist's name. My chop has a crane carved into the top, a symbol of longevity in China, and my name in ancient Chinese characters on the bottom.

A Chinese expression says that while diamonds are expensive, jade knows no price. This is because jade has some extraordinary characteristics. Supposedly, the color—generally red or green—of a bracelet or amulet deepens over time, absorbing some of the qi, or vital energy, of its wearer. If the wearer becomes ill, the color lightens, reflecting the owner's diminished health.

Jade is fragile, but a person should not worry if it breaks, for the jade will suffer for her.

After lunch, we headed for the terra cotta army. They alone are worth the trip to Xi'an. So far, there are two main halls, the second of which is about the size of two football fields in length and packed with the clay soldiers. Not one soldier is the same as the next; the details on the figures are all individual, as they would be in life; faces are unique even to the ears and equally unique is the armor, dress, headgear, shoes, and all else. This was the army that was to accompany Qin Shi Huangdi in heaven. More astonishing still is that the excavation is far from complete. The archeologists have yet to determine how the artisans made so large a host with such individual characteristics.

Outside the entrance to the terra cotta soldiers, a shop sells small reproductions of the soldiers, cards, and other souvenirs. I chose to buy a book that relates how the army was discovered and includes photos. My book was signed by one of the two farmers who unearthed an artifact that led to the excavation of the army.

Xi'an has other notable features. It has a large Muslim population and a mosque. The city is known for its needlework, and Nell and I bought some examples to take home. The work was both intricate and lovely as well as expensive. We also sampled a bowl of soup, a regional dish that I believe has its origins among the Mongolian population and features mutton and small bits of dough; it was a hearty dish, tasty, and very filling.

Another special treat was a gift from our tour guide. She knew I was interested in calligraphy and so gave me a private tour of shi lin, or the stone forest. This museum contained numerous examples of different styles of Chinese characters, chiseled into large slabs of granite; they served as standardized examples for calligraphers.

All in all, Xi'an proved to be a wonderful excursion.

(Note: Huangdi is the title of China's mythical emperor, the Yellow Emperor; Qin's title, if read in English, would read: Qin is the Yellow Emperor.)

THE "BEST" SCHOOL

I often hear Yang Yan talk about the "best schools" in Changzhou. In the Mao years there was no talk of best schools. People lived in "work units"; they were housed in the same apartment buildings, and their children went to the school that was part of their unit. Undoubtedly, some of the living quarters and schools had differences, but choice was not an option. Some of that changed once Deng Xiaoping became China's leader. One of those best schools was the International School in Changzhou, a private school that catered to the children of affluent parents. Since these are only children as well, they are quite spoiled.

One evening, Anushka, Alex, Sylvia (visiting from her school), and I went to visit the council members who were now the foreign experts at the International School. It was very obvious that the foreign teachers at the school were also spoiled. The four of them were housed in a private home complete with three baths, two washing machines, two sitting areas with televisions, spacious bedrooms, a modern kitchen, and a lovely dining area. The floors were all tiled. Additionally, all four girls were given new bicycles, so they would not have to walk the short distance from the house to the school.

Another school to which Alex, Anushka, and I were invited had boasted of having a "zoo." The zoo turned out to be a number of stuffed animals behind glass cases. In the science room, all of us were startled to see a full-term male infant preserved in a glass casing. He was part of an exhibit on the development of a fertilized egg to a full infant. There was also a full-term female similarly displayed. I think what made this so startling was that those two preserved infants looked ready to be scooped up and hugged. This school, too, I believe, was a best school.

There are ways now around placing a child in a best school. One, of course, is money, and parents have been known to bribe principals. I heard of one case where a parent had promised a principal a van, and when it was not forthcoming on the day school opened for the year, refused to admit the child. The child remained without schooling until the van was supplied. Another way a child can obtain admission to a best school is by doing exceptionally well on an entrance exam. Yang Yan's son, who aced an entrance exam, was given free tuition for four years at Changzhou's best high school. In this case, such schools maintain their reputations for excellence; it's also obvious that they hire a good teaching staff and have excellent facilities. This is not unlike independent schools in the United States, which take good lower-income and minority students but rely on wealthy parents to maintain the school.

THE LITTLE MARKETS AND SHOPPING

About a ten-to-fifteen-minute walk from where I live, there is an open-air market which sells more kinds of foods than you or I care to think about. The street is lined with vegetable booths, generally supplied by local farmers and a tad worn from their trip to the market, most often in open carts, which gather the dust of the streets as it comes from the country. Here, I can find everything from lotus and duck's blood to various greens, bamboo root, potatoes, apples, kiwis, bananas, and oranges. Behind these stands and along the side streets are the fish and meats. Fish, fish heads, turtles, shrimp, eels, and crabs are displayed in small tubs of water. Hens, ducks, pigeons, and sparrows are crammed into cages along the side streets. The meats—mostly pig—are butchered in a sheltered area, and it is no myth that every part of a pig is used except its whistle. Recently, one of my teaching colleagues saw a skinned dog hanging from a hook, although dog isn't a typical Changzhou dish. Snakes, too, can be found in open-air markets, but so far, I haven't seen any in my market. If the sights don't bother you, the smell surely will.

Changzhou has many open-air markets, although not all of them are as large as the one near me. There is also a large open-air market in Beijing, which, according to the television news, will be closed down for reasons of health. China is concerned about people's health. Contrary to what the *New York Times* reported some time ago, AIDS is mentioned on television, and in Beijing, I met a young woman who was involved in AIDS education and prevention. How AIDS is contracted, however, is not part of the information given on television. As for drug use, homosexuality, or prostitution, none is openly admitted. China television news also reported an increase in lung cancers and heart disease; the government advised people to be careful of their health but did not advise people to stop smoking. Smoking among men is widespread in China, so heart and lung disease will continue to increase.

But back to food shopping. Just about the time I arrived in Changzhou, a new supermarket opened. Here, everything is packaged in cellophane, put on ice, or refrigerated, and although many things remain unfamiliar, sanitation seems to prevail. Happy, too, for us foreigners, aisles and many packaged goods are labeled in English as well as Chinese. My favorite label is "inflating foods." I played around with that for a while, and I invite you to do the same, but actually it simply means dehydrated foods that grow when put in hot water. Here, I find the Chinese shoppers very interested in what I put in my shopping cart, and one day, several of my fellow foreign teachers heard a loudspeaker announce: "Foreigners in aisle six." This supermarket, because it is more Western, and so, considered modern, is what Beijing now wants in the city.

Meanwhile, Liu Hong, one of my young faculty, has fallen in love and manages to turn every assignment into a tribute to his new girlfriend. She is, of course, very beautiful and has large lovely eyes. The Chinese are very romantic and fall in love at first sight and, like many of the heroes in their folktales, often die of love—at least, figuratively. Loving someone creates problems; marriage ages for men and women often depend on their place of employment. Boys and girls simply sigh away their love for each other until they reach the requested age. At the same time, people here are very affectionate. There is little touching between males and females, but boys feel free to walk with their arms around each other's waists, and girls walk holding hands or arm in arm. My women students often link arms with me, and one asked one time if she could give me a hug. To my Western eyes, it does seem unusual to see two men in army uniform with arms around each other, and I often wonder what reaction this would create at home. I enjoy this easy affection and sometimes think Americans would be a lot healthier if they could display their caring as easily as people do here. The end of a semester nears, and as at home, this is a very busy time. I doubt I'll have time to write again before I leave for home.

THERE ARE NO SECRETS IN CHINA

There's a saying here that there are no secrets in China. Here, everyone knows my age, and there is scarcely a thing about any of us foreign teachers that the entire campus doesn't know. But if there is a downside to having everyone know more about you than your mother ever knew, there is a plus as well. Since a bout of bronchitis keeps me coughing all the time, my students not only inquire about my health but supply me with hints and things to make me feel better. The student's mother who invited the four of us teachers to lunch has sent me tea eggs—eggs boiled in tea—and is making me a pair of Chinese slippers to keep my feet warm.

I am interested in the Chinese erhu, a violin-like instrument with a long neck, two strings, and a sounding box akin to a medium-sized can. It's played with a bow and has a rich, plaintive sound. I discussed this one day with one of the teachers here and shortly after received a call from someone I had never met and didn't know. "Delia said you like Chinese music," the voice said. "We would like you to come to my house for dumplings, and I will play music for you." This kind of invitation comes frequently here.

It is customary to bring a small gift for your host; anything too expensive or elaborate would be considered rude. I checked with Yang Yan about a proper gift to bring the family and decided on fruit. I discovered that apples and oranges are welcome but not pears, since the word for pears combined with another word has a bad meaning, whereas apples and oranges contain syllables that mean good health and good life.

I have had to give up my tai chi lessons because of my bronchitis but have filled in the time with calligraphy. Gregory, one of my third-year students, has several certificates in calligraphy, and I asked him if he would teach me. I was taken to the campus calligraphy association room and was welcomed by all the members as well as invited to participate in a calligraphy competition. Well, every competition has to have a loser, so if I can manage to come up with a few decent-looking characters, I might just do it. One student also made me a lovely painting of flowers to take home, complete with calligraphy. The characters I am learning to paint are "China American friendship" and are lovely to look at when done properly. I unfortunately like the ancient characters, which I found are the most difficult. I think they are also the most beautiful and, like many of our typefaces, have graceful thicks and thins. Everything about calligraphy, from the proper way to hold the brush to the drawing of the elements of the characters, has a specific name and order for making a character. Ideally, when proficient, my entire self should be one with the brush. One writer has described the movement of the brush as being akin to ballet.

This weekend I am off to Suzhou to take in the sights, meet with friends, and shop for silks.

A POLITICAL LESSON

I have had my first taste of Chinese bureaucracy, and although I was prepared for it, I did not know how even minutia could become a major question. So, to begin...

I participate every Tuesday evening in the English café; this is a student activity where the students can converse in English with the foreign teachers. At one café, I asked about student newspapers and wondered if there was a student-written English publication where English majors could share their poetry and stories. I knew better than to mention articles for fear something political would show up. Anyway, the students were interested in starting such a publication, and I offered to help them with the writing. I then checked with Yang Yan about procedure. She got back to me a day or so later to tell me she had spoken to the president of the university, and it was a no go. Such a publication would have to be okayed by the local council and then by the provincial government in Nanjing and after that, I suppose, by the officials in Beijing. The president was also concerned that the publication might fail—students could lose interest, or the next foreign teachers might not want to work with the students on a paper, which would mean losing face. So, there we had it. Yang Yan and I agreed that I could run a writers' workshop; the students could make a presentation of their works at a campus lecture session, and the best work could be displayed on the school bulletin board. This was fine with me, as I simply enjoy working with the students.

Even if my original project had been okayed, the back and forth among the officials would probably have taken as long as my stay here. It is difficult for new things to begin here, and the roundabout procedures can stifle initiative before it even begins. The experience certainly gave me an interesting insight into the way China works. Even the insignificant can become a major question.

In downtown Changzhou, there is an enormous billboard with Deng Xiaoping's face and a slogan that reads, "Construction is an absolute principle." I believe this actually should be translated as "a high priority."

Several students here play ping-pong with me and seem surprised that a grandmother can compete fairly well. It's fun and I always draw a crowd—who giggle. This weekend, we have been invited to another official banquet. I am to sit at the head table—why? Because I am the oldest foreign teacher, and as an elder, I receive priority (I guess I'm an absolute principle of sorts). I just hope my chopsticks work well for me this evening; there are days when, like tennis, the game goes well, and then there are the days when nothing works.

MY CHINESE STUDENTS

My Chinese students always want to know what American students are like. I tell them I see little difference. Neither American nor Chinese students sit in the front row of the classroom, and neither raise a hand to volunteer to speak. Sometimes American students don't turn in their work either. Still, my Chinese students are far politer than any American students I have had in recent years. I am usually in class five to ten minutes before my class actually begins; students request permission to enter if I am already there. They stand up when called on for an answer; they apologize if they feel their work isn't sufficient; and if I want better behavior, I only need to say that I am disappointed.

A typical college classroom, consisting of two rows of desks with seats. Here, half my class of freshmen in the Tourist Program.

There are several different types of universities and colleges in China. Some are run by the state, such as Beijing University, which is also considered one of the most prestigious here. Others are run by the provinces or cities. Jiangsu Institute of Petrochemical Technology was originally funded by Sinochemical, primarily as a research and engineering school. This is no longer true, and JSIPT is now trying to broaden its curriculum, having recently added an English major. Like many American colleges in the early seventies, Chinese colleges and universities are under threat of being closed if they are not sufficiently comprehensive schools. JSIPT plans to offer a Chinese major in the future, and it now has a tourism program, a wise choice, as tourism in the next several years is predicted to be the number one industry in the global market.

Before a Chinese student can apply to a college or university, he or she must take an examination and pass it. Choice of schools depends on the score; therefore, the best students wind up at Beijing University and other prominent universities

Getting my classes here has been chaotic. I believe I mentioned in previous notes that I arrived at JSIPT two weeks after my business-writing class was to begin. I taught them for a week, and then they were off to visit a factory. I taught them another week, and then we broke for the National Day vacation. For my young faculty class, I had to interview all the applicants to see if they had sufficient English for the class. This class began the week the business students were off to visit the factory. Two students don't belong in this class, but one I accepted because he is a big man on campus, and it would not be politic to refuse him, and the other got in by error. As for my other class, conversational English, this began only after I returned from National Day holiday. This class began late because it is composed of freshman, and first-year students have a month to six weeks of military training before they begin class. Fifty-four students were placed in this class; I figured that if each one spoke during my two-hour class, he or she would have exactly two minutes to talk. I persuaded the business department to break the class into two sections and won major points with everyone because I was willing to teach two more hours. This adds up to twelve teaching hours a week. I may also be teaching kindergarten children at a local primary school; this, however, is a separate story.

Getting class rosters, knowing what books will be used, finding out where the class is located are all last-minute. The scheduling at the school is not computerized, and often one department doesn't know what the other is doing. Another problem I face is that students, even those who have fairly good English, have difficulty hearing and speaking. As a result, I often mime words or draw pictures on the blackboard. My drawings are understood but also are a source of amusement.

Students in China have been brought up to read, memorize, and regurgitate. They sit for hours at a time in lecture halls, where I once witnessed teachers reading to the students from a textbook. Success is passing the examinations, not thinking critically. My challenge is to break through this regimen and make them think critically. As an aside, I see American education becoming more like China's: test scores have become the be-all and end-all; information is not something to be used but something to be memorized, tested, and forgotten. Meanwhile, my fellow teachers and I are teaching the Chinese students to think. This can mean using information to solve a problem and learning to evaluate and analyze information. In my first days teaching the business class, I received homework on scraps of paper or on sheets torn from notebooks. It took me some time to realize that homework, apart from memorizing material in their textbooks, was a new concept for them. They also did not think it important since grades are usually based on test scores. I found myself teaching what I had learned in first grade: name, date in the upper-left-hand corner of a page, and using a full, clean page from a notebook.

I found my business students totally unprepared to write business letters, so I am teaching them the

English composition course I taught at home. They love it. Even when their English has some of the peculiar construction of Chinese English, I am rewarded with lovely sentences, such as these that came from student visits to one of the college gardens: "Willow tree with its long hair drooping like a shy girl." "The bamboo trees are so dark green that the color seems to float down like liquid ink." And "A willow tree waves in the wind, like a slim young girl dancing on stage."

My young faculty students take care of me. When I was overcome with coughing in several classes (Changzhou pollution), a student brought me pang da hai, a traditional Chinese medicine that eases congestion. In this class, I often read Chinese poetry in translation—it's surprising the lessons that come from this, and now one of my young faculty brings both English and Chinese versions of the same poem, so I can hear the Chinese. Students give me new words with each class, and they laugh at my pronunciation. And I laugh at their inability to pronounce "th," which almost always comes out an "S" sound. So, I have some people here taking deep breasts, sank you very much. And they laugh when I explain what some of their mispronunciation means.

A last word. I met Jon Fazzone in Shanghai, and yes, Mother, he looks well; his apartment is lovely (and very clean and orderly); his Chinese progresses, and I had a lovely afternoon in his company. We were both ready for something American, so we wound up at an Italian restaurant, where we ate mice fra diavolo—just kidding. It was great Italian food.

A LETTER HOME

Dear family and friends, this is about my trip down the Changzhou Canal. The canal is part of the Grand Canal that once stretched from Beijing to Hangzhou in southeast China. In Beijing, the canal was covered over, but what remains is still a major waterway for shipping goods north and south in the interior of China. The Yangzi, of course, is a major waterway from east to west.

The four foreign teachers here at Jiangsu Institute were invited to join the university's English majors for the boat ride and conversation. I can't say I saw much of the canal, because I was too engaged in talking with groups of charming young students. Now, I must backtrack a moment before I tell you about my conversations. In China, women ask their husbands or parents for permission to do things or go places. Sons, too, will seek permission from their parents. Most women who are grandmothers have been married, and as I have written elsewhere, there are no secrets in China. People know I have daughters and grandsons. In China, people do not adopt children. Those of you who know me will realize that explaining my life circumstances would be quite an ordeal, so...on to the boat ride.

My first major questions came from a group of boys who wanted to know if I believed in God. I said, maybe, if I had shaken her hand, I would believe in God, but since that had never occurred, I could not say I believed or disbelieved. Well, how did I celebrate Christmas? I told about the tree, the presents, Santa Claus, and family gathering. Well, then, I must believe in God. I asked them if they really believed there was a lady on the moon with her pet frog and rabbit. No. Did they celebrate the Moon Festival with their families and friends and eat moon cakes? Yes. That, I explained, was the same for me and Christmas.

Soon after we got religion out of the way, I was cornered by a group of young women. They asked about my family. I told them about my two daughters and two grandsons. Did I have a cat? I once had a cat, but it died. Did I have a dog? I once had a dog, but it died. What we really want to know is about your husband. Did they want to know how I met him? Oh no. I saw I was soon going to be in the middle of a cultural swamp, so I said very sadly that my husband had gone the way of the dog and cat. They didn't blink, and I got the picture—my charming young students wanted to know about sex. (Religion was so much easier.) They didn't ask any of the other teachers because they are unmarried, and in China, marriage is supposed to comes before sex. All of these students must complete school before they can marry, as it is their parents' wish, and a parent's wish is a child's command. So, it is body and hormones versus school. I commiserated with them and said this was much the same as when I grew up.

Well, to finish this, I believe "raging hormones" must be the most frequently looked up words in their English dictionaries. I have sworn Yang Yan to tell everyone I have lost my husband and it makes me very sad to talk about it.

There are just no dull days here; love and hugs all around.

SHANGHAI

Shanghai—that city of intrigue, mystery, hidden dangers, and foreign concessions, where brothels abounded and children were sold for sex—is now rid of its foreigners and most of the other evils for which it was once infamous. The city has a population of 14.2 million, a fact I mention because Shanghai also has one of the cleanest subway systems I have ever traveled on, putting the Paris metro, the London underground, and the New York subway system to shame—and, I suspect, even the Moscow subway, competition between China and Russia as it is. Not one candy wrapper, ground-out cigarette stub, fruit peel, gum wad, or wayward newspaper can be found on its beautiful tiled platforms or even on the train tracks. The trains themselves are just as clean, and the station restrooms are immaculate.

Like most subway systems at rush hour, however, getting on and off a train is all push and shove. Just as the Chinese seem to demonstrate their individualism driving on the streets, so too do they demonstrate the limits of Chinese patience when boarding or exiting a train or bus. Elbows out and shove! The rush of incoming passengers often prevents the passengers who want to exit from leaving the train. My travels on the Shanghai subway reminded me of a tragic story a Chinese woman wrote for my composition course when I was teaching at home. She grew up during the Japanese invasion of China. When the air raid sirens sounded, all the people in her town took shelter in nearby caves. She and her family as well as several others were in a separate cave, as the men in these families held high-ranking army positions. The other cave served to shelter the rest of the townspeople. This cave was very crowded, and on hot summer days, breathing was difficult. One day after the all-clear sounded, the people in the large cave began pushing to get out. The planes, however, unexpectedly returned and began bombing again. Between the people pushing to get in and those pushing to get out, nearly everyone died, either from bombs or from being trampled.

But on to happier things. My trip here was in quest of textbooks for the faculty class, and I was there with Guan Chunying, one of my faculty students and the college librarian, and a student there to help carry the books. I asked to come along because I wanted to see the Shanghai art museum. So, after book-buying and lunch, I treated my companions to the museum and had the wonderful experience of introducing them to the place. Shanghai's museum is one of China's finest art museums. Set in the gardens of People's Park, the museum is built in the shape of a "ding," an ancient pot, and is handsome both inside and out, with a large tiled terrace leading to the main entrance and marble floors within. Exhibition halls display Chinese pottery, calligraphy, bronzes, jade work, paintings, seals, and ancient coins, all arranged chronologically, with signs in both English and Chinese. I hit the pottery exhibit at the right time on this visit and was rewarded with a demonstration of pottery-making. Pottery is made on a wheel; the potter straddles the wheel and turns it by hand. The room also holds several models of kilns, and these all have names. The egg kiln is oval-shaped, and the dragon kiln—my favorite—climbs up a hillside and is quite long; the model itself is easily fifteen feet long. Kilns are fired by wood. After watching this potter work, I found it easy to see why some Chinese writings refer to God as the Great Potter.

Outside the museum, on another visit, I witnessed another art form. On the terrace outside the main entrance, people were dancing. Apparently, one person brings a CD player and music, and for an hour or two, anyone who wishes comes to dance. If a woman hasn't a partner, she will often dance with another woman or dance alone until some man asks her to be his partner. Squares in many Chinese cities are frequently used for dancing and tai chi or other exercises. Anyone who wishes may join in the exercises, as I did one weekend when I visited a friend in Nanjing. I happened on a tai chi class just as it was finishing, and Mr. Wong, a retired teacher and the leader of the exercises, welcomed me and explained much about tai chi. I told him I had begun lessons and I thought tai chi was very beautiful. He invited me to join his group the next morning. I did, and I was welcomed by the whole class. Mr. Wong said his class was very pleased that I thought tai chi was beautiful and that I wished to join them for class. I told him many things in China were beautiful, which he repeated to the class. Happiness all around. Perhaps I shall return to the States at least knowing my left hand from my right.

THE WAIBAN AND MY HAIRCUT

Probably the most important ingredient in a foreign teacher's happiness in China is her waiban. The waiban is the man or woman who takes care of all the governmental paperwork, helps the foreign teacher settle in, and generally has a command of English. I began to learn how fortunate I was in my waiban when I arrived in Beijing and discovered I was the only one of 126 teachers to have heard from my waiban, who had not only emailed me a greeting before I left for China but had given me information about the school. Yang Yan, our waiban at JSIPT, not only has an excellent command of English but goes the extra mile in helping the four of us here. She arranges our trips to other cities, tells us where the best fruit dealer can be found, introduced us to a woman who hand-knits wool/silk sweaters for about six dollars each, tells the vendors how much they can charge us, and so on. Yang Yan is quite a lovely-looking woman in her early forties, dresses immaculately and stylishly—she has her own dressmaker—and has a good sense of humor as well. Our mothers could not look after us with more care and concern.

Yang Yan's latest service for me was taking me to her hairdresser to have my hair cut. Ms. Liu, said Yang Yan, has experience cutting foreigners' hair, which I should know is quite different from Chinese hair. So, off I went for my hair cut, figuring that the wonderful thing about hair is that it grows, and if I disliked my cut, I had only to wait a month for all to return to normal. This, of course, became another adventure. The entire shop staff turned out to watch my hair being cut, and

I believe they did not miss a hair. Meanwhile, as Ms. Liu cut away, she, Yang Yan, and the staff carried on an animated conversation, which Yang Yan later told me about. First, they noted that I had big ears. Now, before those of you with pink, shell-like ears laugh at my big ones, you should know that big ears are a sign of longevity. The staff also thought I had a big nose; the Chinese think all Westerners have big noses, and big noses have no value other than to amuse the Chinese. The staff wanted me to oil my hair and felt I should color it, because that would make me look younger. Happily, they had already guessed me about ten years younger than I am, so who knows, maybe I should have my hair colored. The haircut, by the way, was excellent.

A few days ago, as I left my classes, I was greeted by three young women who asked if they could talk to me. I said, of course. "We never see a foreign person before, and we are afraid. But we think you are nice," the bravest of the three told me. I assured them I wasn't a bit scary and invited them to come talk to me any time they wished. Chinese students are wonderful and open with their feelings, and I have a collection of things they have written me that would make many of my colleagues green with envy. "I think you must become our good friend. I remember you make us laugh forever," one boy wrote in his paper introducing himself to me. Again, "I want you to like China and

Chinese. Welcome to come with us, Professor Pat."
And my favorite, from Amy: "I'm very glad to know
you, and I'm pleased with your teaching. You are very
kind, just like my granny. You know, in China, teachers
and students are only the teachers and students. They
are not friends. I feel sad about that. But I must obey
the rules. But your class is lively and interesting. It can
draw my attention easily. I want to practice a lot and
pleased to answer your questions or talk with you."

The important part of this last note is that I am like her
granny. Being old in China is not just a matter of respect;
many of my students were raised by their grandmothers, and the bond is very strong. Yang Yan was raised
by her grandmother, and she once told me that she has
little feeling for her parents compared to that for her
grandmother. China, as many of my students constantly
say, has a one-child policy. Even so, many of these only
children are raised by grandparents, as their parents
must both work, some in separate cities. Family life isn't
easy here. In the primary school where I go every other
Thursday to work with the children, ages five through
ten, the children are all boarders, as both parents work.
I wonder how the very little ones cope with being away
from home. A teacher told me that the children cry at
first, but then they are very happy. I wonder. Still, for
all the pleasant comment my students made about my
"granny" attributes, I was also a kind of wonder. "In our
country," a student wrote me, "many old people stay

at home after retirement. But Professor Pat, who may be my granny according to her age in our China, came to China alone. It is very marvelous." I was to learn at several different times that I had become a model for old age.

One-child policy has some curious effects on that only child. The child is spoiled, particularly if he is a boy. Yang Yan told me that when she first came to JSIPT, students came to the college on their own. Now, however, parents have enough money to accompany their child to the school. Students who are only children enjoy being at college as it is often the only place where they meet many people their own age. In the dormitory, rooms that have a minimum of four people sharing a space and, in some dorms, eight people, the only child must share. The problems some of my students tell me about, however, have a familiar ring: someone wants to study when someone wants to sleep; someone hogs the washing facilities, plays music too loudly, always studies and won't play. Still, dorm life gives these only children a taste of cooperation and a sense of other. Although we don't always think so when we're growing up, having brothers and sisters is a benefit to our personal growth.

I expect to be home in Sherman for about six weeks during Spring Festival before returning to Changzhou to complete my teaching contract. See you soon.

THE CHINESE HEART—
AND STOMACH

A student has lent me a book entitled "The Spirit of the Chinese." There is no copyright date in the book, but from its content, I assume it was written sometime between World Wars I and II. The author, a Chinese, writes an abundance of clichés, but one passage is worth passing on, and that is that the Chinese lead with their hearts. I see this every day with my students, with Yang Yan, with my young faculty, and often with those Chinese I meet by chance. If my American students said things to me such as "We all like you, Professor Pat" or "We want to be your friend," I would be very suspicious of their motives. Here, however, the feeling is genuine, and if students have another agenda, it is to speak and practice their English, and that, of course, is why I am here.

This past weekend, all four of us foreign teachers were invited to lunch at the home of Gu Yun, known to us as Mimi and the student who runs the English café. What a groaning board; our dinner could easily have rivaled a Thanksgiving dinner. We began with a series of salads, followed by fish, pork, and vegetable dishes. Then came our silverfish soup, and just as we thought we were about to burst, we were informed that there were "snacks" to come. Our snacks included spring rolls, both vegetable and meat; "jiaozi," or dumplings, again both vegetable and meat; steamed buns; and fried tofu. All of it was delicious. Our student's mother invited us all back to teach us how to make dumplings. According to one of my fellow teachers, guests are always served dumplings, but if you are invited to make them, you are a member of the family. I really enjoyed the student's family, and I hope to learn to make dumplings.

Tonight, I am invited by one of my young faculty for a dinner. This will also be a "groaner," and I am constantly amazed that with all the Chinese eat, they aren't all fat. Still, with what I eat, I am losing weight. I can't think of a better way to live—eat heartily and stay thin, every dieter's dream.

A CHINESE HOSPITAL AND CHINESE MEDICINE

A cold has provided me with another adventure, this with Chinese medicine. My antibiotics didn't seem to do anything for an upper respiratory infection. These are quite common in China. The Chinese blame their chest colds on the changes in the weather; since the weather is very much like that in Connecticut, where I don't get colds, I blame it on the pollution. There are days when I can feel the dust and coal particles getting into my lungs. But, be that as it may, the cold needed attention, and I finally surrendered to Yang Yan's insistence that I see a doctor. Did I want Western or traditional Chinese medicine? I said that since this was a Chinese cold with a Chinese germ, I would go with Chinese medicine.

There are two hospitals in Changzhou: one is Western and one traditional Chinese. As with hospitals in the United States, it's pay first, see the doctor later. However, to see the doctor cost just six yuan, or about seventy-five cents. Follow-up visits are one yuan. I received a booklet saying I had paid and describing my illness. Yang Yan then took me up to the second floor, where I was to see her cousin, a doctor. Along the way, I noticed several rooms designated for acupuncture (and I believe Yang Yan won't let me leave China without a go at acupuncture), diabetes, ultrasound, Western and Chinese medicine combining, and so on. (This last—"and so on"—is how many of my students end a sentence when they run out of English words; I shall have to teach them the glories of "et cetera.") In the doctor's office, I placed my booklet under a stack of booklets and then sat outside the office waiting for my name to be called. I was an object of curiosity to the Chinese patients waiting with me.

When I saw the doctor, she felt my pulse, checked my throat with a tongue depressor, had a look at my tongue, and inquired after my bowels. That said, I was prescribed several medicines. This is the expensive part of the hospital—170 yuan, or a bit more than twenty dollars, which is a lot of money here. I now take three medicines: one is a dark-brown liquid that I drink with warm water, something like tea. It has an interesting taste. My second medicine is a pill, which I take three times a day after meals and has no taste. The third medicine is dark brown, comes in plastic pouches, and must be taken three times a day, between meals. It tastes awful. I have no idea what is in these medicines, and I don't want to know. The Chinese use many herbs and animal parts in their medicines, and I keep thinking of the witches in *Macbeth* and "eye of newt." No matter, I am getting better. Once the cold is gone, I shall be given herbs to restore my "qi," which is my vital energy, and return my body to a normal balance. My body may return to its normal state, but I believe my mind will never be the same.

A LETTER TO MY COLLEGE COHORTS

Dear Colleagues, let me tell you how semesters begin here and how faculty are treated. As you know, I left the States on August 26 and had a week's orientation in Beijing before coming to my teaching post in Changzhou. I arrived to find that my business-writing class had been scheduled to begin on August 28, but that was okay. For another class—young faculty who must learn English—I had to interview them before the class could start. I began that class last week. My third class won't begin until after the National Day holiday, which means the second week in October. My teaching hours won't be more than ten a week because I have papers to correct and my class is twenty-one students. In short, classes begin "whenever."

The students are wonderful. When I met my business-writing class for the first time, the students all applauded, and when I greeted them in Chinese, they applauded again. I generally arrive early for class, and if I am already in the classroom when a student arrives, he or she will ask permission to enter. I have had to stop them from standing up every time they are called on. On my second Saturday here, the university had a teacher appreciation day and several of my students presented me with a bouquet of carnations. Would you say this is a great place to teach? Besides all this, I am, as I think I mentioned before, paid more than the college president. I am probably the highest paid professor on campus. And since I am also the oldest person on campus, everyone defers to me—including the president. Sometimes, the veneration of my gray head is a bit overmuch; they act as if I might die any minute and are surprised that I run up steps and so on.

In addition to my teaching, I must participate in a club activity—the English café. Here, we foreign teachers spend an hour or two conversing with the English majors and other students who wish to practice their

English. I have interested them in starting an English newsletter, which should be enjoyable. (Don't die, Enid and Sally—it won't be political.) I also have a student I play Ping-Pong with. It's surprising how much of a workout that game can be.

My fellow foreign teachers and I are something of celebrities here. Changzhou, unlike Beijing, Nanjing, and Shanghai, sees few foreigners, so we are constantly stared at. A few times, we thought we were going to cause accidents as bicyclists and scooter drivers kept looking after us instead of looking at the road. Children titter at us, as well as some of the adults. At one restaurant, the entire waitstaff surrounded our table. Too bad if anyone else wanted service. The most-looked-after of us four is Alex. She is a tall, willowy young woman with blond hair, blue eyes, and the peaches-and-cream complexion that so many English women are noted for. She is constantly asked by the Chinese to take pictures with them or to hold their little one for a photo.

My Chinese is coming along haltingly, but it's coming along. I ask my classes to teach me a new word every time we meet. I also am beginning my classes with American folk songs—right now, we're doing "On Top of Old Smoky." Songs provide good listening practice and vocabulary as well as being fun.

Here's a Chinese expression for you: "ma ma hu hu." Literally, this translates as "tiger tiger horse horse," but it means "so-so." I haven't had a ma ma hu hu day since I arrived here.

I am not able to spellcheck this, and since the letters are sticky (I'm at a newly discovered internet café, still waiting for my own email setup), you'll have to decipher for yourselves. Also, please see that Minna gets copies of my emails. Love and hugs all around, Pat.

PS: Sally, if you ever visited the open market here, you'd give up eating.

ANOTHER DAY WITH MIMI'S FAMILY

Today, I ate myself silly at Mimi's house. Her mother invited me for both lunch and dinner, and there were at least seven different dishes. Between meals, Mimi's cousin and her cousin's friend came to interview me for a report they are doing on education reform. Using more up-to-date teaching methods is one of the goals the government has set for the next five years, and I found it interesting that students were asked to be part of the study that may lead to different pedagogical techniques.

At dinner that evening, I learned that Mimi's mother had lost her grandfather during the Cultural Revolution, and as with so many children and grandchildren whose parents or grandparents were singled out for "capi-talist" leanings, the offspring also suffered. Mimi's mother was not permitted to continue her schooling. Professor Xiao, with whom I played Ping-Pong one af-ternoon, said he was an English major in college when the Cultural Revolution occurred and so was sent from college to work in a factory. He apologized for his English, as so much was lost before he could return to school.

There were so many other stories I heard about that period. Yang Yan's grandfather lost his life in prison only to be "pardoned" after his death. Qiong, my professor of Chinese cultural history, lost her grand-parents, small landlords killed by local peasants. Her mother, therefore, lived under a cloud. A Chinese cal-ligrapher I met was forced to divorce his wife or lose his job.

It was very easy to come under suspicion or be de-nounced for even a minor mistake. My faculty student Helen wrote the following for me:

"There is a story about my father and my sister dur-ing the Cultural Revolution; once, one of my father's colleagues gave a picture of Chairman Mao to my sis-ter, a sacred picture at that time. My sister was very young at the time and she knew nothing about politics. She took out a pencil and scribbled on it and then she put it in the dustbin. In the evening when the workers cleaned the office, they found that picture and they were scared. Finally, they found that it was done by my sister. It was a very serious political problem. My father was nearly put in jail, if it were not for the help of his colleagues. They protected him and he and my family avoided a disaster."

Many young people lost their chance at education. Those who had been sent down to farms and factories were often too old for school once education again became a priority. Older siblings remained as factory workers while their younger siblings continued on to college and easier lives. This was true for Helen and Mr. Wu, both of whom paid for children of their older siblings to go to school.

A FAVORITE CLASS

One of my favorite classes is the young faculty class. This consists of the teachers who either want or need to improve their English. There is also the added incentive of an increase in salary for adding a language to their resumes. The majority of the class has good reading and writing skills and fairly good speaking skills but needs work on listening comprehension, which requires much practice. I begin every class with reading a poem and have chosen Chinese poems translated into English. The poetry introduces new vocabulary and offers a good beginning for discussion. I first read at a normal pace, telling the class to write down as many words as they can hear. I then read very slowly to give them a chance to "hear" more words. Finally, I read again at a normal pace. I ask them about any words they don't know the meaning of, and once we have gone over the vocabulary, I ask them to tell me about the meaning of the poem. They were all quite surprised when I told them the poem I read in English was a translation of the famous poet Tu Fu (Tang dynasty, 618–907 CE). Since I began sharing my collection of his poems, the class has begun to add to my collection. Here, according to my student Helen, is the most famous of Tu Fu's poems, one of the four thousand he wrote.

Cold Rain on a Spring Night

A good rain falling
Just when it should
In Spring time; riding
On the wind it fills
A whole night, soaking
The land with its goodness;
Clouds hang heavily over
Country paths; a lone light
Shines from a passing boat;
Morning, and I see a damp
Redness on the branches,
Laden down with flowers.

My class assures me that this sounds much better in Chinese, and I agree. Translating Chinese poetry into English presents the translator with two options: she or he can try for the rhyme or the meaning. I found the translations that went for the rhyme often lost the meaning of the poem and offered a tortured language in order to rhyme. Chinese poetry has its own rules of composition, lost to those of us who don't know the language. Shakespeare would not fare too well in Chinese.

Helen provided the class with the Chinese originals, and I asked her to read them in the original, so I could get a sense of what the poem sounded like in Chinese. I love Tu Fu's poetry, but my class said his work was too sad. The greatest Chinese poet was Li Bai. I hadn't found anything by him in my anthology, and this turned out to be because he is called Li Po in my books. "Aha!" my students said and informed me this was because the translators did not properly understand Chinese characters. They introduced me to the work of Mao Zedong. Mao was a fine poet and calligrapher, something that gets lost in his political and economic actions. Interesting to me was that the class all immediately recognized his poetry when I read it in English. One of Helen's other gifts to me was a book of Mao's poetry in both Chinese and English. I was also given one of the Little Red Books, a compilation of the Chairman's sayings, carried by nearly everyone and often memorized as well.

CHINESE BIRTHDAYS

Among my young faculty, not one had ever had a birthday cake, although they knew such cakes were now common among young people. On birthdays, the traditional celebration came in a bowl of noodles topped with an egg. The noodles were especially long, as a long noodle meant long life. I imagine for some who experienced the famine of the Great Leap Forward, an egg would have been nearly priceless.

My own birthday is in mid-December, nearing the end of the semester, so I decided to celebrate with a birthday cake in class along with a lesson on how Americans celebrated birthdays. I also asked Yang Yan if she could arrange hot water, so we could have tea with our cake. I then went to the Times supermarket, which has a good bakery, and selected a large cake. The icing included fruit in the decoration and proved, later, on eating, to be delicious. The counterman, who was holding up what appeared to be small fork, asked how many. I thought he wanted to know how many people. I found out when I replied twenty-three, this was not the case, as he placed the numbers two and three on the cake. This made a funny story for my class, and we all celebrated our twenty-third birthday.

The class included Yang Yan, Leona, and the teacher who oversaw faculty studies. There were even leftovers, and one faculty student asked if she could take home a piece for her child; he had never had a birthday cake. It was an enjoyable and good class.

The following week, my faculty students gave me gifts for Christmas. "Should I open them?" I asked the class, and they gave consent. The gifts were Changzhou combs and included not only four of the eight beauties but three Chinese deities: the god of longevity, the god of wealth, and the god of happiness (or good health). This trio always are part of the wish for a long life. It would be cruel to wish someone many years if he did not have the health and means to enjoy them. The combs themselves are known as empress combs because of their artistry. They are a specialty of Changzhou. The city is on the canal that once stretched from Beijing to Hangzhou, where the court often spent summers. On the way was a stop at Changzhou to purchase what were deemed the highest quality of combs. They are still manufactured in the city.

You may have noticed that I asked if I could open the presents. Except for fruit that I gave to my hostess when I was invited for dinner, no gift I gave was ever opened in my presence. This spared the recipient from exclamations of delight and gratitude, perhaps lies, or an expression of disappointment that could not be disguised. If you have ever received a hideous Christmas present from Great Aunt Matilda, you will appreciate this way of doing things. Still, I have wondered to this day if something I gave as a present was liked or not.

SUZHOU VISIT

I'm off this weekend to visit Suzhou, often called the garden city, as it once had more than ninety-three gardens, only several of which survived the Cultural Revolution. The city is about a half-hour train ride from Shanghai and one of the must-see places in China. I shall be meeting up with Nell and Brian and a friend of theirs to tour the city and shall stay in the Suzhou university guesthouse. (An aside, most colleges and universities have guesthouses. They supply clean beds and baths for visiting guests and tourists for a cost much lower than a hotel; additionally, guesthouses are very near inexpensive restaurants.)

The old part of Suzhou features ancient homes and shops, many of them sited on canals. They reminded me of the "mews" in Greenwich Village and seem like a great place to own a home. I think, however, that like Greenwich Village, they are pricey. Within this part of the city are two of the gardens Suzhou is famous for. First is the Garden of the Humble Administrator, which I decided is the kind of humble I would happily be. The garden stretches over several acres abundant with flowering shrubs, ponds, and streams, which create islands and each island area features a building. Some buildings are simply places where a person can sit to read and relax. All in all, a beautiful place to visit..

The second garden home is known as the Master of the Nets. The "master" who owned this house was not a fisherman, but the canal that passed his house was often fished. For most connoisseurs of architecture, this home is considered the most beautiful in Suzhou, mainly because of its use of space. Windows all look out at plantings, which creates a feeling that outdoors lies a great expanse. The inner courtyard has been replicated at the Metropolitan Museum of Art.

Another place to visit is the silk factory, where a tourist can see everything from silk worm cocoons whose threads are waiting to be separated to ancient looms to finished weavings. Suzhou is a good place to buy silks.

With Brian, Nell, and friend, I enjoyed my first milk tea. Along with milk and tea, the glass held small BB-sized black items that we jokingly dubbed "fish eyes." They did not have any particular taste.

The weekend provided a treat from work and also a chance to shop. I decided to take the six weeks of Spring Festival, or Chinese New Year, to visit home. Spring Festival, by the way, is something akin to Thanksgiving and Christmas all rolled into one, with all the family and lots of food and presents.

BACK AGAIN IN CHANGZHOU

My welcome back to Changzhou included a big hug and "I miss you" from Mr. Zhou. Having a hug from a man friend isn't noteworthy at home, but in China that action even among close male and female friends is taboo. I believe we foreign teachers have westernized Mr. Zhou.

Apart from that hug, the semester begins as usual—in total chaos. The term began on February 17, but as most departments have not yet returned, our class schedules haven't been made, so I have a week's time before my classes begin. Yesterday, I thought I had everything settled, but a visit from two of my young faculty makes me think I shall be facing another schedule entirely when I visit the foreign affairs office this lunchtime. There have been other important changes during the holiday break. Classes have been divided into forty-five-minute periods versus the earlier fifty minutes, and faculty are to teach three hours rather than two. The staff are now required to come to work at 7:45 rather than 8:00, have lunch at 11:30 rather than noon, and leave at 5:00. Anyone who has worked a factory production line or had her workload increased because of downsizing will recognize what is going on here. I also understand from Yang Yan that many people were let go. The saddest part of this for us foreign teachers is that Yang Yan has chosen to take another job, which will be good for her, as it makes better use of her abilities, but most unfortunate for us.

This week while I await my class schedule, I have bumped into several of my young faculty. I learned the class had come to the guesthouse to see me off, but I had already left. I am rather glad I did miss them because I think I would have cried at their kindness. Several young faculty have also visited me to tell me our class will run again this term. This requires some explaining, not only of why it is unusual but also of Chinese custom. My students and I both have taken advantage of the Chinese wish never to lose face nor to cause others to lose face. At the end of the last term, I learned that my young faculty were to be given a written test by another college teacher. My class, however, was a conversation class, and there had been no mention that students were to be prepared for a written exam. I let it be known that I was deeply offended, that I had been a teacher for more than thirty years, and I was in the best position to judge my students' work. I felt the school was saying it did not trust my judgment or respect my teaching. The upshot of that was that my students did not have to take a written test.

My young faculty used the same tactic to continue the class another semester. Usually, an English class for faculty runs just one semester. I had told the class that they were doing so well it seemed a shame not to let them continue to learn and to practice. They repeated this to the personnel department and added that I was very hurt that I could not have the class for another term. So, an exception has been made, but not because it makes good educational sense but because they don't wish to hurt me. It pays to learn something of a country's customs before visiting, and this custom has certainly served me as well as it serves the Chinese. Saving face—not only of oneself but of others—is something Miss Manners could add to her book of etiquette.

WOMAN'S DAY

March 8 was officially Woman's Day here in China, and I received a carnation from each of my young tourist classes. My students are very sweet to me, and the day provided a chance to do some cultural exploration on gender roles, so I asked the class how they felt about women having a day to celebrate themselves. They all agreed, young men and women alike, that this was a fine idea. After all, it was Mao Zedong who said women held up half the sky, and whatever else one feels about him, he did a great deal to liberate Chinese women from many of the bonds of tradition.

Why wasn't there a men's day? I asked then. Frowns from the young men in the class; questioning faces on the young women. So, I answered my own question: that's because every day is men's day. Cheers from the men; laughter from the young women. I said that perhaps there would be true equality when we no longer had to single out a day to acknowledge women's contributions to society. There was agreement all around.

I then wanted to find out how they felt about sharing housework. I discovered many of the young men had helped mothers or fathers cook dinner; many had helped clean house and do wash. Similarly, the young women had helped fathers with the housework or with yard chores. I had noticed at Yang Yan's home that her husband often cooked or cleaned up the kitchen, and one evening when all four of us foreign teachers and Yang Yan's supervisor, Mr. Zhou, came for dinner, it was Yang Yan's husband and Mr. Zhou who cleared the table and washed the dishes. I wondered if this shared housework would be alien to my students when they married and had a child, but all agreed that if they and their spouses both worked, the cleaning and cooking would also be shared. In fact, they assumed this would be the case.

Now, add to this that most Chinese men are not only very romantic but also very tender-hearted and they would seem to be the perfect mate. I was, in fact, about to tell American women that if they wanted an ideal husband, come to China; however, the very next day I read an article in China Daily, which had surveyed Chinese men and found that unlike my students, most Chinese men fit right into the old pattern of women at home taking care of children and family. In fact, one man commented on women's natural maternal instincts, which, of course, is why they belong at home. And, naturally, while they are there, they might as well cook and clean.

One glimmer of hope in this was the feeling that women should receive some kind of pay for their work at home.

I have also had my second haircut here, and because the hairdresser who had previously cut my hair was ill and on leave for a month, I went to a hairdresser right on campus. Yang Yan came to give cutting instructions, and Mr. Zhou came along to watch. There was no discussion this time about my large ears and nose; the hairdresser went straight to work, and for three yuan—about forty cents—I had a shampoo, cut, and blow dry. My hair was washed under a faucet and over a sink, not too bad until I was informed by Yang Yan that on my next visit, I should perhaps bring my own towel. It turned out that there was a "shop" towel. The shop would have sent an American health inspector into shock. Apart from the walls, which looked as if they had not seen paint or a washing since Qin Shi Huangdi unified China in 215 BCE, there were piles of hair on the floor and brushed against the wall, enough to stuff a sizable pillow. The socket for the blow dryer was hand-wired, two twisted wires leading from what source I could not discover, and I half expected that when the hairdresser plugged in the blow dryer, one or the other of us would be electrocuted. But no. The haircut is quite nice, I have not found any head sores or creatures crawling in my scalp, so apart from bringing along my own towel and comb on my next haircut, I am quite satisfied. This adventure cost all of two yuan, or about thirty cents.

I have learned once again from my students that although I am old, I have the heart of a sixteen-year-old girl. I didn't want to tell them that at sixteen, I was much older than I am now. Nor that, at sixteen, was I on a balcony with a young man looking at the full moon with a telescope. You, readers, can invent the details of this as you wish.

MAO AS POET

My book of Mao Zedong's poetry in both the original Chinese and the English translation was a gift from Helen Shi. Helen was both a history teacher at the college and a member of my young faculty class. She was also the person who provided the original Chinese of Tu Fu's poems, which I had read to the class in English. She was an invaluable source of information.

One of the history courses Helen taught was on the Cultural Revolution, and I learned that the course blamed it squarely on Mao, whereas the common story placed the blame on his wife. This surprised me, as Mao was still so revered by most Chinese. Helen also had a photo of Madame Mao, one I had wished to see, as she had been an actress, though a minor one. I did not find her particularly pretty. A more interesting photo showed Madame Mao with her first husband and another couple; both pairs were just married. Helen told me most of the photos had been destroyed, as it was not common knowledge that Mao's wife had a previous marriage. The other couple disappeared as well.

For all his later excesses, Mao did much for China. Literacy of the population reached 98 per cent with the advent of free primary schools, he simplified Chinese characters, and in keeping with his statement that women made up half the sky, he said daughters could not be forced to marry a man they did not like.

Among Mao Zedong's poems in the collection Helen gave me is his poem "Against the Second 'Encirclement' Campaign," written in 1931. The poem refers to the battles against Chiang Kai Shek's Nationalists as well as the Long March. Although most in the West know Mao as the ruthless head of Red China, he was known to the Chinese as a great leader, a poet, and a calligrapher. Many Chinese still consider Mao great but add that he was not good at economics—a reference to the Great Leap Forward, which led to the death of nearly 30 million people from starvation. The Cultural Revolution was until recently blamed on Mao's wife, and it will be interesting to see how the Chairman's reputation will fare in future years. Mao liked to compare himself to Qin Shi Huangdi, China's first emperor and the uniter of the country. Like Mao, he introduced many reforms to the country, and like Mao, he was also known for his cruelty.

Mao's poetry provides insights into both the country and the man. Here, from "Changsha," written in 1925, are the young revolutionary Mao and his friends:

Young, we were, schoolmates,
At life's full flowering;
Filled with enthusiasm
Boldly we cast all restraints aside,
Pointing to our mountains and our rivers,
Setting people afire with our words,
We counted the mighty no more than muck.
Remember still
How, venturing midstream, we struck the waters
And waves stayed the speeding boats?

In "Swimming," Mao talks of the future greatness of China:

A bridge will fly to span the north and south,
Turning a deep chasm into a thoroughfare;
Walls of stone will stand upstream to the west
To hold back Wushan's clouds and rain
Till a smooth lake rises in the narrow gorges.

The bridge connects China's north and south and crosses the Yangzi. Until it was built, goods moved across the river by ferry. The Russians were to have built the bridge, but a falling out between Khrushchev and Mao led the Russians to abandon the plan. It was thought the

Chinese could never build it on their own. The Yangzi is treacherous; not only are the currents strong and often unpredictable but the river may rise as much as eighteen feet during rainy periods. The Chinese did build it, however, and tourists to Nanjing will often include the bridge as one of the main sites to visit.

China's second Great Wall that is cited in the poem is the dam, a dream of Sun Yatsen and now a reality. This, like the bridge, is an engineering marvel. The problems the dam may create, changing silting patterns and located in an area known for earthquakes, poses a potential disaster.

In addition to history, Mao's poetry provides an insight into the man. He may be considered China's last emperor, with the same kind of power over people as his predecessors. Emperors were supposedly gifted with some special ability: Many were able military men; others were known for their calligraphy or poetry. Here, from "Snow," written in 1936:

> This land so rich in beauty
> Has made countless heroes bow in homage.
> But alas! Chin Shih-huang and Han Wu-ti
> Were lacking in literary grace,
> And Tang Tai-tsung and Sung Tai-tsu
> Had little poetry in their souls;
> And Genghis Khan,
> Proud son of Heaven for a day,

Knew only shooting eagles, bow outstretched.
All are past and gone!
For truly great men Look to this age alone.

And, who is the truly great man among great men?
Mao, of course.

A FIVE-YEAR PLAN AND A TRIP TO THE ZOO

As part of its next five-year plan, the Chinese government has set educational and legal reforms among its goals. The government here means the Chinese Communist Party. There are, contrary to popular belief, other parties. Yang Yan belongs to the Supporting Party, which has a say but no power and probably never will have. At any rate, this time I shall focus on educational reform. The Chinese feel that education is the key to advancing technologically and have been looking to the West, most particularly the United States, for models.

Some time ago, I was interviewed by two middle-school students—ninth graders in our country—for my ideas. They had been assigned a research paper on improving education, and I was a primary source. I spoke mostly about teaching English and found their English teacher used many of the pedagogical techniques that we used in my college. This, however, is not true at Jiangsu Institute, nor does it seem true of the English education many of my students received in primary and middle schools.

Traditional Chinese education, as I have mentioned previously, is test-oriented. Students are quite good at grammar and vocabulary but cannot speak well and also listen poorly. The English teachers here are superb grammarians; I sometimes follow such a class and am awed by what I see left on the blackboard. Still, the students don't practice speaking what they have learned. I wonder daily why such a grammar/vocabulary class isn't followed by a speaking class. This would reinforce the vocabulary that students learn. Students also don't know how to write typical composition assignments; logical arguments such as we teach in American schools are not part of the Chinese writing experience. Critical thinking skills need much work. I am doing my bit to nudge students into writing and thinking more. It's fun but uphill work.

This Saturday past, the women administrators with their children went to the Shanghai zoo, about a four-hour trip, as the zoo is a considerable distance from that city. We foreign teachers were invited along—all of this as part of the celebration of International Women's Day. Women faculty in each part of the college will be celebrating in whatever way they choose.

The zoo was quite an experience. There is an attempt to have an open range for the animals as in many other zoos but no attempt to prevent people from feeding the animals. The women on our bus fed cake to the giraffes; these were not shy about coming right up to the bus and poking their heads into the windows. In the monkey and goat areas, the keepers sold feed; still, people added cake to whatever else they had brought along for snacks. The effect of some of this feeding was evident on a black bear, whose tongue was full of sores. At the lion and tiger exhibits, a vendor sold live chickens. These were tossed out bus windows to the lions, who then would chase after the buses in hopes of more food.

In part of the zoo, children could have rides on camels, elephants, donkeys, or a horse-drawn cart. Here, too, we witnessed the saddest part of the zoo. People could have their picture taken with a tiger. This animal was drugged to prevent it from attacking, but so it would look ferocious for the photograph, its keeper would hit it in the throat with an iron bar. It's apparent that there are no animal rights activists here in China.

A LETTER HOME

Dear old gang of mine and friends, I had such an interesting chat with a student last evening that I felt I must pass it on. I also want to say in advance that I am working on a keyboard that is sticky from all the drinks and seeds that people eat at the internet café and that has letters so worn from use that I am truly touch-typing, which happened to be my only low grade in high school. So now that you're warned, on to the story.

I am coming down with another cold, and I was looking forward to my nice warm apartment at the end of class—8:00 p.m.—taking just a little time to talk with a young man who has difficulty "hearing" English. The door to the class was open, and two young women popped in to talk to me. One of them wants to be a journalist and, like so many of my breed, had lots of questions. The most interesting were about Falun Gong and what did I think about it and what would happen to members of that group if they were living in the United States. I have begun to feel that for some members of the group it is indeed a cult and a very unfortunate one for the families whose children have decided to burn themselves into nirvana. I'm not sure if the leader of the cult is using the United States or if the State Department is using the cult to buttress its claims that China suppresses religious freedom. Almost every religion is represented here in China, and people do attend churches, mosques, and Buddhist and Daoist temples. A synagogue—a very famous one in the Chinese city that once had the largest Jewish community—was destroyed in a major flood earlier in the nineteenth century and never rebuilt. (There is still a group of Chinese who claim to be Jewish but know little about their faith, and kosher restaurants still exist in some Chinese cities.) Today, many people have returned to their faith and are free to do so. I explained our concept of religious freedom and how we have dealt with cults in the United States, when the would-be journalist said she thought it was wrong to just print that the Falun Gong was bad; media should find out what made so many people join it. Good question. She would like to see more freedom of the press. She said many young people had new and different ideas—moving more toward democracy and choice. People may keep quiet here, but there is an undercurrent that reminds me of something an anthropology teacher once told a class: even in what we consider "primitive" societies, there are the naysayers and nonbelievers.

Sometime soon I shall write about a Chinese professor I have seen interviewed on Dialogue, one of the TV programs in English. Professor Wu Qing has been a leader in reforms of the marriage laws and the treatment of women as well as a district deputy and city deputy in Beijing, and I hope I can have an interview with her before I go home. She is very outspoken on both women's issues and democracy and quite a gutsy woman.

I learned once more that my students think I am a role model for growing old. Love and hugs all around. Pat.

A DIVORCED WOMAN

A Chinese saying: For women, marriage is a chore; for men, a paradise. A divorced woman has an even harder life. Generally, she is left with the child and is both penniless and property-less, as bank accounts and homes are in the man's name. I met Wu Liping through her friend Delia, a member of JSIPT's English department and a friend of mine. Delia, whose Chinese name is Xu Ping, and Wu Liping were longtime friends and had children of the same age: Crystal, the eight-year-old daughter of Liping, and Andrew, the eight-year-old son of Delia. Liping agreed to an interview about her life as a divorced woman.

She was married at age twenty-five. "I was innocent and naive," she said, "both sexually and practically." Her husband was a classmate. She discovered they had different values and opinions. He was disappointed that their child was a daughter, an opinion shared by his mother, who urged him to get a divorce and marry a woman who would give him a son. He became physically and mentally abusive as well as unfaithful. They separated after two years of marriage.

Despite these facts, getting a divorce was not easy. She appeared before the court three times before receiving her divorce. Her union leader testified on her behalf, and a colleague testified to the infidelity. She was left empty-handed and with custody of her daughter. She had neither alimony nor child support.

"I had a good job and the same salary as my husband," Liping told me. "When he began abusing me, I worked harder and made more money than he did." Still, getting started on her own took nearly a year. She and her daughter lived in a relative's spare room for ten months before establishing herself. "I treasure this period of time today," she said, "because it taught me." Still: "I am in a low position compared to other women. Divorced women have a low profile; there must be something wrong with the woman."

Although new laws will help theoretically, Liping claimed they would not help practically. "Men will try to hide their wealth, and women will get nothing. The only power is if a woman has her own wealth."

A divorcee in Changzhou has a lonelier time than divorced women in Beijing and Shanghai, where there are support groups divorced women have organized. Liping credits her daughter for giving her the will and courage to succeed. "Crystal is my proudest accomplishment. Seeing my daughter's innocent eyes, I will not collapse. I will go on with my life. I have no time to sob." Crystal has helped her to mature.

Liping hopes Crystal will not be as innocent as she was. She will teach her to look for someone who is ambitious, kind, and educated.

As for Crystal's father, he has remarried and has a son. He has not seen his daughter since the divorce, nor has he ever contributed to her support.

A TREAT FROM JIANGSU OFFICIALS

Every year, the foreign affairs office of Jiangsu province takes all of the foreign teachers in the province on a trip to a major city. This year, the teachers all went to Xuzhou, one of the many ancient capitals of China. Xuzhou was a stop on the silk road and also served as the capital of many Han dynasty emperors. The dynasty, which lasted from approximately 200 BCE to 200 CE, stands out as one of the unifying and peaceful periods in China's long history. Our tour took us to two imperial tombs, spectacular, as tombs of that period were carved into mountains of stone. The extensive passages and burial rooms were chiseled out by hand, and the chisel marks were evident on both the walls and the ceilings. The hammer and chisel on display were simple hand tools, and it boggles the mind to consider how many people and how long it took to fashion a tomb.

Our treatment during this tour was royal, if one may use that word in a Communist country. Everywhere we went, we were greeted by signs with messages such as "Welcome, foreign experts and scholars" and "Welcome, foreign experts in culture and education." I particularly enjoyed the latter. We also had the police escort us to every site we visited, clearing our way through traffic. I could easily live with this kind of treatment for the rest of my life. For the eating record, I had my first taste in China of frog and tripe. Neither particularly appealed to me, and the French do both much better.

For me, the most interesting as well as the most moving part of the trip came at our visit to a school for the deaf and blind. This visit was also part of a propaganda effort. China smarts at accusations about human rights, and this school was a showcase of the country's concern for human rights—it takes care of its blind and deaf children. (Many of these children were most likely abandoned by their parents.) As all our visits were being televised, I have images of appearing on television as one of the foreigners impressed by China's concern for its people. The school was excellent, and as I have previously worked with a deaf child and taken a course in sign language, I knew something about what I was being shown.

The children greeted us at the school gate with balloons and "huangyi ni"—or welcome. It was clear from the varying sounds that many of the deaf children were learning to speak. I guessed that those whose speech was poor had arrived at the school later than those children who spoke clearly. The children performed for us. A group of seven- and eight-year-old deaf children danced for us, never missing a beat or a step. If you are curious about how the children could keep time with the music, it is because they can feel the vibrations of the sounds from music. Also, one of the teachers signed with them during their dance. The foreign teachers applauded for them, which, of course, the children could not hear. The proper way to applaud the deaf is to wave one's hands in the air. After the entertainment, I checked with the teachers to see if this way of showing approval was also used in China. It is. I exchanged with the teachers and several of the children the way we sign "I love you" in the United States, and they in turn showed me how they sign the same words in China.

There were also performances by older deaf children as well as several of the blind children, one of whom soloed on the erhu. We then toured the school where we saw children doing calligraphy, paper-cutting, painting, and embroidery. The teaching staff and children had a warm relationship, and I was impressed by the caring and the faculty itself.

The day ended magically for me because of a major goof on my part. I visited a display of the children's artwork and fell in love with one of the paintings, which I thought would be a wonderful, happy painting for my grandchildren. I thought the painting and children's crafts were for sale, and I asked if I could buy the painting. Out came the headmaster, off to the art room go countless officials, and back they come with the painting. It is not for sale; it is a gift. I ask if I can make some kind of contribution to the school. No. I compose a wonderful thank you on the spot, all of this being filmed for television, and then board the bus with my painting. For you, future travelers to Asian countries, remember what I forgot—don't admire or offer to buy anything you like if it is not in a store, or the people will insist on giving it to you.

GARBAGE, GARBAGE, GARBAGE

Every morning last semester around 6:30, just about the time daylight was filtering through my curtains, I heard the banging of a pot followed by a cry in Chinese. I recognized the sound of a pot from the days my children liked to play with the pots and pans, but why this ungodly noise broke the day escaped me. I imagined some kind of colonial-era night watch assuring me and the rest of Changzhou that all was well. Sometime later, I caught sight of one of the pot bangers; he was riding a bicycle cart through the streets and calling out for any refuse that local residents wanted to dispose of—and that he could sell. There are several of these scavengers, both male and female, cycling through the streets and local apartment complexes, banging their pots and calling for throwaway papers, metal, and plastic. I have also witnessed men and women going through trash baskets to collect plastic water and drink bottles; these can be turned in for cash, and I have several times been approached by people begging me for my water bottles when I have finished drinking.

Such is China's recycling program. Garbage is a problem here. Apart from what people throw away in the streets and on buses and trains, waste is piled in any convenient depression along walls or beside roads. The daily sweeping by shopkeepers and street cleaners disappears down drains in the sidewalks and streets but has no place to go. I suspect that most garbage finds its way into the local canal. At one canal a short walk from our guesthouse, there are several boat people who live year-round on the canal.

Few fish could survive the water in this canal, so what these people do for a living or how they survive the seasons remains a mystery. What does remain obvious is that they live on their own garbage heap. Trash is littered on top of the boat, stashed in a depression near their boat, and lined against a nearby wall. At one time, there was a small Pekinese dog tied to the boat, a sorry animal whose coat was matted and filthy. He most likely lived on scraps and possibly served as a rat catcher. I have not seen him this term, so he either died or was eaten.

The garbage piles I see in Changzhou I also see in other towns and villages. There is, in short, no efficient waste management here, part of the pollution problem the country is trying to solve. The sewer system, too, needs updating; human waste disappears into streams and rivers as does factory waste. Tap water in China has the potential to kill; everything here is boiled, and potable water must be bought. My students are amazed that I eat raw vegetables at home and that I can drink water from my tap.

I am not certain that the news of a factory explosion here was reported at home. Several people were killed and many injured. The authorities said a bomb planted by one or more disgruntled workers caused the explosion. He or they were among several thousands who lost jobs in a recent layoff. This kind of report is surprising. Generally, news of catastrophes isn't aired. It also points to the government's concern for stability here. The farmers—about 70 per cent of China's people still work farms—are dissatisfied because they haven't shared the prosperity of urban areas, and as the country moves toward modern management and technological innovations, more workers will lose jobs. As this explosion makes apparent, dissatisfaction of these two groups poses a real threat to stability. It will be interesting to see how this country can manage both to modernize and maintain stability.

Reform of the legal system is one of the goals for this next five-year plan, so the study here in Changzhou is one of many being done on prisons and reforms. China has moved forward on many human rights issues, perhaps not the way human rights are considered in the West, but small improvements, and it is a shame that the country hasn't been given the credit it deserves for what it has already done and what it is trying to do.

A MEETING OF WOMEN JOURNALISTS

China Daily, one of several Chinese newspapers published in English, recently carried a story about a meeting of women journalists and women farmers. The meeting was something of a consciousness-raising session for both, akin to the groups American women formed in the late sixties and early seventies.

Approximately 70 per cent of China's population are farmers, and a good part of farm work is done by women. The figures quoted by the paper are worth citing:

"According to the 2000 China Statistical Yearbook compiled by the National Bureau of Statistics, out of the total rural labor force 46 per cent were women in 1999. But according to the All China Women's Federation, out of 320 million rural labourers who do actual work in the fields, 65.6 per cent are women.

"More than half of the country's gross agricultural product is contributed by women, according to the All China Women's Federation. In the world, about 1.6 billion women work in the fields, contributing to agricultural production, and teaching centuries-old farming skills to the young, according to a United Nations report."

The journalists at this meeting acknowledged that the story of women farmers was an underreported story. As one woman farmer commented, she thought newspapers covered only famous people. For the women farmers, many changed their opinions about a woman's place being in the home. One had been forced to leave school in primary school, whereas her four brothers had all been sent on for further education. She decided her daughter deserved an education. Another realized she knew as much about selecting and planting seeds as her husband. She would, in the future, also select seeds.

Here, at Jiangsu Institute of Petrochemical Technology, a new women's dormitory is being built to house the additional women students expected in the fall. As in the United States, more women are enrolling in universities, and the effects of this will be curious on the government's recent announcement that men's pay will be raised so that women can stay home. The government also wants to see a return to Confucianism, mainly because of its emphasis on order. Confucius, however, definitely put women in a secondary position, both in the home and in the social order. How this will all square with the increased education of young women will be something to watch these coming years.

Among my young students, both men and women feel a woman should work if it makes her happy. One young man offered that he would be delighted to stay home and do the housework and take care of their child—echoes of the "house husband" that arose in the States in the seventies. In jobs, the "glass ceiling" exists as it does in the States, and I joked to my class that both China and the United States have yet to elect a woman president.

Marriages are no longer arranged here; rather, romantic love has become the way young people choose their partners. This has led to an increased divorce rate, and again, as in the States, women suffer most from divorce. They generally have custody of the child (more than one child is highly unusual here), whereas the husband comes away with the money. Divorced women are looked down on, have a difficult time finding work, and are generally impoverished. Spousal abuse presents another problem, and currently the government is attempting to remedy both the plight of divorced women and spousal abuse. Beijing has a women's hotline. One interesting wrinkle in all this is that employers prefer to hire married women who already have a child. This has nothing to do with employer benevolence; women who have a child while they are employed can have up to a year's leave and their job must be reserved for them—a rather pricey business expense.

Some other things American and Chinese women share: the standards of what makes a beautiful woman. I have many women students write such things as "I am not a beautiful girl, but I am a lovely girl," and, "I am not a beautiful girl, but I am a clever girl." This last comment, Yang Yan told me, has its place among Chinese sayings—that a girl is born either beautiful or clever. (I asked her how she came away with both, to which she just smiled.) The "beauty" standard is set by actresses and models just as it seems to be worldwide. Girls whom boys don't find pretty are called "dinosaurs"; unattractive boys are called "frogs." There is no mention that these frogs ever become princes.

As for me, I am busier than ever. On Wednesdays, the business faculty who sit in on my class take me to lunch, and several business department members have promised to teach me Chinese card games. I have a weekend date with the English department, whose members have suddenly taken an interest in me. I have ping pong dates with one of the administrators and the physical education teacher, who promised to show me how to deliver killer shots in exchange for teaching her some English. I already have the Chinese faculty in the ping pong room saying "good shot," "luck," and "bad shot." I also run an extra conversational English group for students who want more practice, and one of the school guards constantly corners me to speak English. I have taken to sneaking by the school gate, so I won't be trapped for an hour or so. Still, how can you refuse someone who says, "I will remember you forever"? Other than all this, if George Bush thinks he has difficulty with China, he should try the character in calligraphy. Then again, America is also difficult.

THE AIRPLANE INCIDENT

As you can imagine, one of the hot topics here is the downed Chinese aircraft and the invasion of Chinese airspace by the United States intelligence gathering plane (read, "spy"). Apart from student questions in the classroom, I have experienced no unpleasant moments—that is, until yesterday. I was waiting to cross the street with several Chinese friends and another foreign teacher when a man on a bicycle stopped before us and began haranguing us about America. Even with my basic Chinese, I could detect the constant angry "Meiguoren" and "Meiguo." My Chinese friends were embarrassed for me and told the man to shove off. He eventually did. In class, I have said if I were president, I would apologize—and, in fact, would have done so immediately rather than make an apology a "face" issue. (My students are ready to elect me president—that's 1.6 billion votes, and even Florida can't offset that.)

Just a few random notes to follow up on the news: Chinese television is declaring a triumph over the plane incident, claiming that the United States apologized and that the plane crew was sent home for humanitarian reasons. The news also claims that the situation is still not resolved; from what I have gathered from the home papers, the United States won't back down on surveillance flights, a source of much anger here. Partly, the anger is due to Chinese sensitivity about its own place in the world; partly, this has to do with what I gather is a military buildup along the coast (I doubt that the country is planning an invasion of Taiwan). United States–bashing also comes across in the long segment given to the race riots in Cincinnati, with facts and figures on income disparity, the number of blacks who serve as judges, the disproportionate number of blacks in prison, and—very amusing to me for its singling out of Bill Gates—that only five hundred of the twenty thousand Microsoft employees are black.

China, on the other hand, respects its minorities. I believe the Uighurs and Tibetans would disagree.

I personally think it's an error to create bad Sino-American relations, but then, I'm not Secretary of State. So much of the news at home focuses on the human rights issue—which certainly leaves much to be desired by our standards—but I feel the media are missing a really important story here. In one of his books, Tom Wicker noted that the press had missed one of the biggest stories of the decade (the 1960s): the migration of black farmers from the South to the North, one of the largest migrations in history. Here, while we bait the Chinese, they are forging relationships throughout the world—both economic and cultural. President Jiang Zemin has traveled throughout Southeast Asia, Latin America, the Middle East, and Africa, signing trade agreements. In every press conference, he and the leaders of other nations express their "one China" policy and, although indirectly stated, their opposition to United States hegemony. United States hegemony is a popular theme here; the Chinese resent America's imposition of its values on China, and they have a lot of support for their attitude in other parts of the world. The big threat of China is that it will become an economic powerhouse.

Although there is much hostility toward the United States, even the Chinese would not buy the recent claim in a Japanese history book that World War II was caused by United States aggression. The history book, soon to be used in schools throughout Japan, has created a real furor in both China and Korea. The Chinese resent that Japan has not acknowledged or apologized for its army's atrocities in WWII, most specifically the rape of Nanjing, and the Koreans hate the Japanese for refusing to acknowledge forcing Korean women to serve as "comfort women." There have been demonstrations and flag burnings in both China and Korea.

On Saturdays when the weather is pleasant, I meet in the little garden with any students who wish to practice conversational English. I had heard about students paying off professors, and this Saturday asked my group if this was so. It seems that if a student fails an exam, one to two hundred yuan (about twenty-five US dollars) will get a passing grade. This does happen at my school. The student will learn the professor's phone number and address or go to the restaurant where the professor takes lunch every day and either directly or indirectly through the restaurateur offers the professor money. I was told that one student who paid a professor to pass denounced the teacher to the college president once he had graduated. The teacher was not fired, just denounced to the college community. Salaries here run about nineteen hundred to twenty-two hundred yuan a month, less than US$300, so it's easy to see why a bit of extra money comes in handy. No one has attempted to bribe me, but that is because I make a princely salary by Chinese standards.

I am going to have a suit made for me here, more reasonable than anything I could buy at home. The handknit silk/wool cardigan I had made cost me all of sixteen dollars, which included the material. Hard to beat prices here.

THINGS THAT AREN'T WHAT THEY SEEM

I was reading in bed one night when I heard the familiar *pop-pop* of fireworks, and sure enough, when I looked out the window, I saw brilliant bursts of red, green, and white lighting up the night sky. I hadn't recalled hearing of any particular holiday for that day nor had my students mentioned any celebration. The "holiday," I learned the next day, was actually an explosion in one of the chemical labs, an experiment gone wrong. No one was hurt, but the lab was seriously damaged.

There are many things, such as the "fireworks," that are not what they seem here in China. Ms. Dong is one of those things. Ms. Dong is the dean of the English department. She is a woman in her late forties or early fifties, short and a bit plump, and all smiles. For those of you who have seen *Raise the Red Lanterns*, Ms. Dong is Second Wife. I had originally been slated to teach in the English department, but Ms. Dong nixed it—she didn't want such an old teacher. That did not endear her to me, but I was quite content to be teaching in the business department and especially so as I had heard the English department was a difficult one.

Therefore, I was quite surprised when I received a call from Ms. Dong one evening asking if I would help her find the meaning of a word. It was the only word in the film *Pride and Prejudice* that she did not understand and that did not appear in the dictionary. Would I come and watch the film with her and see if I knew the word?

Now, this seemed a rather odd request to me. How important could one word in an old film be? Something else was afoot, and I was curious to see what the game was. I said I was happy to see what I could do. So, off I went to the English department to watch one of the old makes of *Pride and Prejudice*.

The word "aversing" doesn't appear in a standard dictionary, and after checking out the words "aversion" and "averse," I informed Ms. Dong that the word seemed to be used ironically in keeping with the dialogue. The word itself may have been invented by the script writer or an old form that could be found in the Oxford English Dictionary. Was she familiar with that collection? I asked with a sweet smile of my own. Of course, she wasn't, as I was certain she would not be.

Profuse thanks and an invitation to join her in her office for some tea. "I hear you know about many things," she said. Another smile. "And here is something for you. A little gift."

Now, that really surprised me. A gift for a word? I protested. She insisted. The gift was an articulated fish and rather handsome. Ms. Dong said the fish had a deep meaning in China, and I told her that it also had a meaning in the West. For the first time, I saw her startled. What was the meaning? I explained the symbolism of fish in Christianity, the miracle of the loaves and fish, the Sermon on the Mount. There were elements in the Sermon on the Mount, I offered, that even Karl Marx would be sympathetic to. Oh, said Ms. Dong with relief, she was afraid the fish might be a bad symbol. I hoped she would go crazy trying to find the parallels between Marx and the Sermon on the Mount.

"And now," Ms Dong said, "maybe you could tell me about this." She whipped out a paper from her briefcase; it was a translation from Chinese to English. Was it okay? I zipped through the translation and made some suggestions. Not much work. Another smile from Ms. Dong. "Do you mind if I call you again?" she asked.

I had been outwitted after all. The present was a contract for help with future translations. I could not refuse now. Ms. Dong would be paid handsomely for her translations, for which I had received a fish.

"I told you," said Yang Yan. "Let me see the fish." I showed her my gift. She made a face. "I have one like that. It's much bigger."

MY STUDENTS' COMPLAINTS

There are twenty-seven students in my oral English class, all of whom are accounting majors. Not one of them wants to be an accountant. Here, in China, test scores determine a student's major as well as which college he or she will attend. One of the accounting students would really like to be a doctor but did not score high enough on her tests. Among my young faculty, few hold degrees or teach in subjects that they would have chosen if given the choice.

The tests Chinese students take are national, and it is quite common to see students at all times of the year pacing up and down in our college garden, book in hand, reciting aloud what they are reading. This is how they memorize their texts, and a good memory will earn a good test score. Students must take six to seven such tests each semester; right now, my business administration students must take a level six English exam. "You cannot get a good job if you don't pass this test," a student said. Yet they have little time to prepare for such an exam, as it is scheduled at the end of a semester during regular exam time.

Among the things students wish to change about their education, testing heads the list. After that, they would like the chance to choose a major and to have some practical job training. They might be surprised to learn that many of their teachers agree with them.

Testing as it is designed is a poor way to judge individual intelligence. Among the hierarchy of thinking skills, memorization is lowest, and this is what most tests test. The ability to evaluate, analyze and then synthesize information ranks among the higher thinking skills, but these are difficult to measure by an objective test. Apart from the order of thinking skills, studies have shown that within twenty-four hours, most students will have forgotten 50 per cent of what they have memorized for a test! After several months, the amount remembered decreases to somewhere around 15 per cent. In the States, many colleges have discovered that the best predictor of a student's academic success is his or her high school academic performance. Another study done in the States showed that although American students in the lower grades perform relatively low compared to students the same age in Europe and Asia, they outperform them in college. Some educators credit this to the way American students are taught to think. I mention all this because testing seems to be taking over American education.

My Chinese students do a lot of thinking, but I doubt the system will ever discover this without major changes both in the classroom and in freedom of expression. For instance, one course my students hate is politics. This involves a study of Marxist, Leninist, and Maoist thought. "It is boring," one student said. "It is out-of-date," another student said. Their reactions to what they read are not part of a classroom discussion since student insights and thoughts have no place in exams. I find an undercurrent of opinion here that remains silent. "There are some things we don't like to say," another student said. (It was Kant who said an idea not expressed is not an idea.) Many authoritarian governments find freedom of thought dangerous, but not allowing it can also be dangerous. As my would-be journalist said, why doesn't the government try to find out why so many young people are attracted to the Falun Gong? There are many such good questions turning over in students' minds. I suspect many of those questions also exist in many other minds. It will be interesting to see how they play out as this younger generation comes of age.

A LAST CALLIGRAPHY CLASS

Tomorrow, I have my last calligraphy lesson. My teacher, Shen Guohua, is a student in my business-writing class and has several certificates in calligraphy. "It would be an honor," he said when I asked him if he would teach me. I'm not sure how much of an honor he now considers it. Our lessons are a combination of praise and good-humored ribbing. "I think you must do everything well," he said one time. Another time I heard, "Well, you are now as good as a middle-school student." A middle-school student is a seventh or eighth grader.

Other times, he just laughs at me and says I have invented my own style of calligraphy. Occasionally, I hear a compliment on a particular character. About a frustratingly difficult stroke, Shen has told me that it is even difficult for a Chinese.

I enjoy watching his brush dance across the paper as he forms the characters he is helping me learn. He has taught me a lot about the art, which has given me insight into the varying styles of calligraphy. Even more, he has taught me another way of thinking. He once said that when he had a difficult day or was troubled about something, practicing his calligraphy made him calm. Practicing does indeed clear the mind, the way a good brisk walk or a fine recording does. Characters demand total concentration; ideally, I am to become one with the brush. I must hold the brush in a proscribed way, varying the pressure as I make each stroke in its specified order. Although calligraphy is so disciplined and structured, it offers a great feeling of freedom and serenity. I know that on the days it is too cold or wet to walk, I have another outlet for clearing my mind.

Both art and philosophy unite here. Freedom comes from making oneself totally a part of what one is do-ing. Going with the flow describes this best and has the randomness associated with much of modem physics. The Chinese story of the butcher who never had to sharpen his knife is an example. He had learned where the spaces were between the bones and so his knife never became dull. He did not have to cut or hack.

Leaving here makes me sad, but at the same time, I look forward to seeing family and friends, to eating salad again and swimming in the lake, to tending my garden, and to attending the Sherman Chamber Ensemble con-certs. Of course, a bit of veneration from everyone will help ease my transition from East to West.

BUSY LAST WEEKS

These last weeks have been so crammed with activ-ity, my head is spinning. A good thing, too, because I waken every day now feeling sad as I contemplate leaving. My university "lends" out us foreign teachers;

local middle schools and other colleges also want native English speakers, so these schools constantly ask for us to lecture. This week, I gave a lecture at the Wujin Television University, and I'm scheduled to give another next week. The university has nothing to do with preparing students for careers in television; rather, the courses are given over the tube. In addition to my lectures for this college, I have another hour at the primary school and a presentation to give here at my college. My presentation here will be all about Sherman; students are interested about life in America, and I thought a small New England town would be something new and different for them.

Apart from this, I spent a weekend in Nanjing. I met for a farewell dinner with several of my friends from the Council, the organization which sponsored us in China, and we had a rousing good time. I came back to my hotel room in a student dormitory to find the power had been cut off and so had to climb nineteen flights of stairs to my room. I was in great shape for this as I had recently climbed Yellow Mountain—about five miles of stairs—and stopped to rest only for the young concierge who was lighting my way with a flashlight.

Nanjing is now a modem city and, of all the cities I have visited, appeals to me most. On this visit, my second purpose was to visit the museum that documents the massacre in that city during World War II. More than 300,000 people were slaughtered by the Japanese, who entered the city in December 1937. Soldiers who had surrendered were rounded up, gunned down, or used for bayonet practice. The river actually ran red with blood. All the elderly and young men were also gathered to be killed. An estimated twenty thousand women were raped, usually gang-raped, and most were then killed. Although Buddhism is also part of Japan's religious heritage, the Buddhist monastery was raided, the monks killed, and the nuns raped. Often, the Japanese beheaded their captives, and there was one report of a contest between two Japanese soldiers to see which of them could behead one hundred people first. When their killing was a draw, they then decided to continue until their victims numbered 150. Most of the photographs in the museum were taken by Japanese soldiers, and the account of the soldiers' killing contest was reported in Japanese papers.

Although the massacre was reported in Western papers, much of this information was quietly "forgotten" as the United States built up Japan as a bulwark against Communist China. Less well-known are the experimental camps where the Chinese were used to test germs, used to test survival in extreme conditions, and used as guinea pigs for various drugs. The Japanese called the Chinese "logs" and, since logs have no feeling, were known to have dissected children while they were alive and unsedated. It is little wonder that the

Chinese are outraged at the new Japanese history book to be used in schools, which claims no responsibility for World War II nor admits to atrocities. Fortunately, there is a group of Japanese historians who are also protesting this history book.

Now, to lighten up a bit. My students at English café have taught me a few Chinese hand gestures, several of which are very rude. In turn, I taught them a few Western gestures. When I showed them the finger sign for "cuckold" used in Europe, they told me that in China, there is a saying instead: "You wear a green hat and have small shoes." Don't ask me to explain how that means a man's wife is unfaithful to him, because the Chinese students couldn't explain it either. As for the middle finger used in the States, the Chinese raise their pinky—it means the same thing.

HOMEWARD BOUND

It's hard for me to believe that I shall be leaving Changzhou. I have made so many dear friends here that I leave with a heavy heart and something of a sense of amazement. I had expected that with such a profound difference in language and culture, it would take me some time to feel comfortable in China. Yet I seem to have simply slipped into life here without more than an occasional pause—such as at the outdoor market near our school, filled with all sorts of strange and wonderful sights and odors; with the free-for-alls getting on and off buses and trains; and with the chaotic beginnings and ends of every semester, as well as the challenge of crossing the street.

Still, I note I have changed some here, and the biggest change for me is how I feel about the market. I have come to love that place, crammed with foods, farmers, countless little shops that sell everything from shoes and underwear to woks and batteries. I can buy fabric here and go to any one of many tailors to have a garment made or stop by a knitting supply booth and have a sweater knit for myself. I can even go to the dentist here, as I noted the other day as I passed by a man having work done on his teeth right at the side of the road.

In the large cities, modern supermarkets are replacing many of the small shopping areas. Here, a customer can pick her choice of fowl for dinner.

*Open air pork market; pork and chicken
are the major meats in China.*

Turtles, eels and fish heads are kept fresh in tubs of water.

Fishmonger scales fish and guts frogs for sale.

A customer can find anything she wants from vegetables to sweaters to batteries in the market. Here, the morning crowd of shoppers.

Vegetables and fruits can be found on one of the side alleys, some biked in from the countryside.

I enjoy going in the early morning when the street is crammed with old mothers buying their day's food, farmers in from the market with vegetables and fruits, and where I can buy my breakfast as I walk along. Some days, I opt for steamed buns, doughy rounds filled with vegetables and meat or sweet bean paste. Most days, though, I go for another kind of cake. These are a phyllo-like dough filled with bean paste or vegetables, rolled in sesame seed, and lightly fried. The shapes indicate whether the filling is vegetable or bean paste. I have also taken to buying tea eggs. These are hard-boiled eggs cooked in a broth of tea and soy sauce. Very delicious, as my students would tell me. Occasionally, I stop to buy some roast duck for my dinner. I can order a whole or a half and then watch the butcher neatly hack the meat to bite-sized pieces with his cleaver and arrange all artistically in a carry-out box. Yes, there is take-home in China.

Although the Times, a modem supermarket, is a lot more sanitary than my little market, it has acquired many of the consumer-beware packaging of United States supermarkets—there is certain to be at least one squishy whatever in the cellophane-wrapped package. I also like trying to bargain with the farmers for my vegetables and recently tried some strawberries.

It is generally not safe to eat uncooked food, but Yang Yan told me if I washed the strawberries, soaked them in a little salt water, then rinsed them with clean water, they should be safe to eat. They were, but a bit salty, as I hadn't been told just how much salt was proper.

This week, I saw a number of snakes for sale at the market. The Chinese like snake meat, and they must like a lot of it. I understand from a recent television program that the snake population is diminishing to a point where ecologists are worried. Though I prefer snakes at a considerable distance from myself, I do appreciate that they eat other undesirable things. Still, I can't actually cry for them. I did wonder, however, if perhaps St. Patrick, who rid Ireland of snakes, might simply have been a hungry Chinese.

I still struggle with my calligraphy and Chinese. The former is improving, but the latter has far to go. I was very proud of myself for learning to say "so much rain"—we had a few rain-filled weeks. But if you remember, Chinese has tones—use the wrong one and you wind up saying something fairly stupid. So, what I said was "such a big fish." After my students finished laughing, I learned the correct tone. One down and thousands more to come.

I shall miss my students and my Chinese faculty friends. In a matter of hours and an ocean, I shall no longer be a foreign expert nor shall everyone defer to me because of age. Television cameras will no longer tape my every move and gesture, and there will be no police escort to clear my way through traffic. On the one hand, I shall miss this, but on the other, I welcome being an ordinary mortal once again.

CHANGZHOU
2002–03

ONCE AGAIN IN CHANGZHOU

I am again teaching at Jiangsu Institute of Petrochemical Technology in Changzhou. When my students wrote about JSIPT, they always said, "Our college is a small college." At the time, it had five thousand students. When I left the school a year ago, a new women's dormitory was being built, and the administration expected the school to grow to six thousand by the fall. That dorm is complete, a bit more handsome than the usual gray dorm buildings, and it is just a small part of the expansion the college expects by next year.

"You won't know this place, Pat," Yang Yan wrote me before I came. And although this is not quite the case, the growth here is extraordinary. First, the college is building a new campus in another part of the city; enrollment for next year will be ten thousand. The main thoroughfare in Changzhou has been widened, making crossing that street even more of a challenge, and all along the road, new apartment buildings are sprouting up. Many of the small shops along our street have been demolished to be replaced by apartments or other stores. Two open markets remain, including the one I have always loved, but now there is a hospital a few blocks from campus featuring both traditional and Western medicine. There are countless new restaurants: an elegant one right around the corner from our rooms, a fantastic dumpling place, a Muslim restaurant, and a "hamburger" shop. "Hamburger" here means chicken. And don't ask why because I can't answer.

My fellow teachers this year include Michelle and Peter from England and Julia and Phil Smith and Marija from the United States. The British contingent is young and taught here last semester. The others are older—mostly retired—but I remain the most venerable. Our semester begins the first of September—more or less. Several classes won't meet for another two weeks as the students—freshmen and sophomores—have military training.

Yes, I am happy to be here again. I had a big hug from Mr. Zhou (we foreign teachers have westernized him about hugs from women), and even the receptionists and staff in our dormitory have given me a wonderful welcome, a bit surprising as I always felt they didn't care for any of us. Yang Yan has revolutionized her appearance as well—gone is the wavy perm replaced by perfectly straight hair with a mod cut. She looks even younger than before.

Despite the changes and growth, the feeling remains, and I look forward to my classes and new friendships.

A SEMESTER BEGINS

Classes begin next week. This week, I have been settling in: getting my courses and schedule; meeting my co-teacher and members of the English department, for which I teach this year; and setting up my rooms, which this year includes a washing machine. The most important part of this week, however, belongs to officialdom. Foreign teachers must have both a residence card and a work permit, and this information goes first to the Security Administration in Nanjing, then to Changzhou officials. The cards look like small passports and can be used in place of a passport when we bank or reserve hotel rooms. Everyone in China has both residence and work permits—the workplace determines residency, part of Mao's wish to keep the country people in the countryside and city people under watch. Even so, many farmers come illegally into the cities looking for work, and with so much construction going on in Beijing, Shanghai, and even Changzhou, these workers can supplement the family income with wages from construction. Having a place to live, however, is hard to come by.

Changzhou's continuing boom—the city is one of the industrial development zones—has made the city richer but has also increased crime as workers from the countryside come here to find work. Bicycles, the main means of transportation in China, are a prime target for thieves, and several people I know have had more than one bicycle stolen. I am sure we must also watch for pickpockets.

My classes this year include three writing courses, one oral English course, and one class on American and British cultures. I have been reading a book on the United Kingdom to refresh my college English history course and came across the delightful reference to Robin Hood as England's first socialist hero. The translator has done a wonderful job on the English, but it is clear from several passages that there is a definite slant to the information about both the United States and the United Kingdom. This course should be fun to teach.

I have also been seeing many old friends here. Xu Ping, one of the English teachers whom I came to know last year, invited me for dinner at her home and then took me to dance exercises in the square by her home. This group meets at five-thirty every morning, first for some tai chi and then to dance. They meet again at seven in the evening, a group that I have been joining on a regular basis so far. One of the joys of China is joining in on such an activity. The place where we dance also has basketball hoops, so there are always boys dribbling or chasing basketballs between the dancers. Some of the little girls try to follow their mothers' dance steps, pausing only to look at the foreign woman's strange Western face.

Our dance class begins with a round of warm-up exercises, followed by several dances. The movement is gentle but does involve legs, arms, and torso and like one of the forms of tai chi is great for balance and overall stretching. Our dance instructor is a retired physical education teacher at the college; my classmates are women of all ages (I believe, however, that I am the oldest) and varying abilities. I am happy about the latter while I try to sort out the steps—it seems just as I am getting the hang of one thing, the teacher changes the step. I doubt that I'll ever be good enough to do these dances with fans; in the morning, the women add fans to their dancing. This is quite lovely to watch—also to hear as the fans snap open then close as the steps and rhythm change.

I'M INVITED TO A WEDDING

I am not certain if any readers remember Liu Hong, the young faculty member of my English class who managed to turn every assignment into a tribute to his new girlfriend. I understand he may marry on National Day, October 1. He would have been happy to marry earlier, but China encourages later marriages, and his girlfriend was too young in 2001. If he had married her, although legal, his workplace—the college—would have penalized him, possibly by refusing to let him teach here any longer. The marriage laws and one-child policy are still in effect. Chinese population has decreased, but the country still has not reached its goal of a permanent population of 1.4 billion. Farming families may have two children, and the minority populations—there are fifty-six—have no restriction on the numbers of children they may have.

My wedding invitation came in a bright-red card, red being the color of happiness and success. It also came with a small box of sweets, the box, too, a bright red and tied with a pink ribbon and bow. Sweets are traditional as they invite the relatives and friends to participate in the sweetness of the day. In earlier times, the sweets came in the form of sweet buns; today, it is candy, quite a bit more expensive but fashionable.

The day before the wedding, I was informed that as a guest of honor I would be required to make a speech. Few Chinese weddings, I was told, have foreign guests, not to mention an old (venerable) foreign guest. I would be seated right next to the family's table. The morning of the wedding found me in the library with Guan Chunying, another member of my faculty class and an invaluable friend. We were to go over what I would say. She wanted to make sure it was Chinese enough. Actually, there is little difference in wishes for a couple here or at home: a long and happy life together. I also asked for a few Chinese words to say at the end of my speech. In Chinese, the wish is: "bai tou shi lao; bai nian hen hao."

This translates roughly as "May you be together until your hair grows white, and may those years be very happy."

Everything okayed, Guan Chunying and I headed for the Hailun hotel in the center of town. I believe there were at least twenty tables set up in the hotel dining room, and though I was told there were to be 140 guests, I felt there were at least two hundred. In the back of the room, the wall had been decorated in bright red; two pink hearts were set in the center, flanked on either side by the Chinese characters for double happiness.

The wedding banner at the reception featured two characters for "double happines"

The bride wore white, a new fashion among the young Chinese. After the ceremony, she changed first to a long and traditional red dress and again to a shorter red dress. I did prefer the red dresses. The ceremony included a traditional drinking of wine together and demands a bit of acrobatic ability. Each partner must wrap his or her arm around the neck of the other, glass in hand, and bring it to the other person's lips to drink. It makes a clumsy way to drink, but it certainly brings the couple together in a tight embrace. Having emptied their wine glasses, the couple was pronounced man and wife, and the guests clamored for them to kiss—not traditional. At first, Liu Hong kissed his new wife on the forehead. This did not satisfy the guests, nor did their kisses on each other's cheeks. A Hollywood kiss was in order, so blushing bride and bridegroom finally obliged. Then, the father of the bride made a speech, followed by my speech. I think my Chinese was okay.

If ordinary banquets have more food than a guest can eat, a wedding banquet has enough for an army. Most Chinese banquets begin with a number of small dishes: six to eight. On our table, there were at least a dozen—fish, cucumber, chicken, duck, beef, pork, beans, and others that I can't remember. This was followed by a soup, then the fish dishes—shrimp, stuffed clams—and pork, duck, and chicken. In between came puff pastries, a sweet rice, and stuffed buns. Last were a number of vegetables followed by a whole fish and a whole steamed turtle. The whole fish is traditional, and I remember seeing a Chinese film where the family was too poor to provide a real fish, so they had a wooden fish served as a token. The turtle is for longevity. A chicken soup and sweet rice ended the meal. All the time the guests ate, the bride and groom were making the rounds of the tables and toasting.

Western white bridal gowns are now popular in China

The bride later changed into a traditional red dress

The last part of the wedding included something akin to the bride and bridegroom feeding each other wedding cake. Here, the couple had to eat a rather glutinous rice ball from one spoon—again bringing them close together. That done, the wedding was over.

The next day, Liu Hong appeared at my door. He had come to return my wedding gift. In China, the custom is to give money—about three hundred to five hundred yuan is considered good. Five hundred yuan is generally what a relative gives, so I settled on the three hundred, after checking with Yang Yan to make sure it was a satisfactory gift. It is important to be generous but not ostentatious. Liu Hong told me it was an honor to have me for a guest, and I should not have to give a gift. I said it was an honor to be invited, and I was happy to give a gift. This went back and forth several times, and then I remembered something I had read by Confucius about gift-giving —after the third time of my offering, it would be appropriate to accept. So the third time around, I told Liu Hong to please keep my gift, and all I would like in return was a cake from his wedding banquet for his family, to be held in his home village over the holiday break. He promised me a big cake.

NATIONAL DAY CELEBRATION

October 1 celebrates National Day, which is the founding day of the People's Republic of China. The day begins a weeklong holiday, and it is one of the times I really regret not being fluent in Chinese. All this week, television shows present biographies and documentaries on Mao Zedong and Zhou En-lai, the long march and the fight for control of China. The other evening, one channel showed a film based on the journalist Edgar Snow, author of *Red Star over China*. Snow was one of the few reporters to actually interview Mao and to report on the Red Army. I could follow about a fourth of this film, as a fourth of it was in English; the remaining three-fourths was guesswork.

Changzhou, as I mentioned in my earlier notes, is booming. The main road has been widened enough to include bicycle paths on each side, making life much safer for cyclists. I would no longer be afraid to ride a bike into town. A traffic light has been installed at the corner, making crossing the street less of a challenge, and the bus station has been paved and repainted. No longer do I get off the bus on a rainy day and step into a water-filled pothole. Everything is looking spit-and-polish. The old gray apartment buildings along the street have also been repainted and now sport a pink/beige color; the new apartments going up come in a variety of colors. Changzhou's new buildings resemble some of the elegant high-rise apartments in Shanghai.

Changzhou apartment houses generally come in drab gray. Most are six stories high and have no elevators;

they are poorly maintained. Halls and stairwells are dirty, there are no lights, and if there were, no one has the responsibility for replacing them when they burn out. So, it comes as a surprise to walk into a fairly elegant apartment with tiled floors, a modern bath, and good furniture. Many of the college faculty own their apartments. In some cases, the college helps with the financing, and the faculty pay mortgages. They also pay a one-time tax to the government based on the price of the apartment. There are no common charges in most of these apartments; the most people pay is a small fee for a security guard. In new buildings, common charges are added to mortgage payments. These charges take care of maintenance and security. There's nothing drab about these places.

The widening of the main street hasn't eliminated the marketplace I enjoy so much. It is still crammed with old mothers buying the day's vegetables, young mothers buying clothes for their babies, young and old men buying breakfast breads, and it still smells of the fish, vegetables, and cooking that take place in the stalls that line either side of the small alleys. My latest discovery is a place where I can buy fish or pork balls, both of which make wonderful soups. I have been joining my fellow teachers cooking here in our kitchen; Julia, who came here with her husband and is Chinese, has been teaching the rest of us the art of the wok and Chinese seasonings.

I have been giving my students English names; some of them already have given themselves names. Among them are Ice, Rain, Chopin, and Benz. (Yes, that's Mercedes-Benz because, as its owner noted, Benz was the best car, and he wanted to be the best man.) But the best name I have heard belongs to a young woman who has called herself Willing.

CHINESE STUDENTS COMMENT ON AMERICA

I asked my students in the American culture class to write everything they knew about the United States, good, bad, and indifferent. They did not have to include their names, so their responses are quite candid. Chinese students know a surprising amount about the United States: they cite it as being the fourth largest in land; as having one of the world's great rivers—the Mississippi; and as having five Great Lakes. They can name many of our largest cities as well as some of our outstanding universities, Harvard, MIT, and Columbia among them. They even comment on the improvement of the United States soccer team in the World Cup matches. Almost all students commented on this country's superior technology, economy, and military power. Here follows some of their ideas about the United States:

"America is well-known as it's advanced in economy, military forces and almost every field. That is, America is the only superpower in the world after the collapse of the Soviet Union. So naturally, America plays an important role in world affairs. So America is regarded as 'the police of the world.' Frankly speaking, sometimes America is just overdoing."

Another student responded, "The United States has 50 states. It's a children's heaven, youth's battlefield and aged people's graves." A classmate noted, "America is said to be a country lived on wheels." Another wrote, "For most people, the U.S. is a fairyland…But I think it is for the rich people. For the poor people, life there is very hard."

Our eating habits came into question. "Why," wondered a student, "do American people love to eat fast food while Chinese people pay a lot of attention to diet whenever they are busy? Do American people worry about the nutrition of food?"

Several students complained about Americans' lack of knowledge about China. "American people are industrious and peace-loving," wrote one, "but I think they may be deceived by mass communications. They don't know China well, especially contemporary China. I want many Americans to come to China to learn about China and make friends with China." Another wrote, "I know something about American history because we have learned it from my middle school books. As China has opened its windows, Chinese people care more about the world. But, to my disappointment, American people seem to know little about China. I wonder about whether American people care about the world. At least they don't know much about China, but we know much about America."

Students admire the United States for its freedom and opportunity. "American people are very open-minded, they emphasize individualism. Freedom is the most important," said one. To another, "In my mind, America is a country full of opportunities and challenge." Several noted the freedom of the press and democratic institutions. "In the USA, the press has much more freedom than in China. The newspapers dare to say something adverse to the present authority. They can even reveal the scandal of some important politicians. How do they manage to do that? Can't they be punished in some way? As you know, in China it is prohibited. If someone does that, I can't imagine what the result will be." Another student said he frankly liked America. "I like the sense of freedom and democracy in America." Still another wrote about the United States, "Most important, it has a sound democratic and legislative system."

Comments about the current administration, however, are harsh. "Many Americans win our respect such as Washington, Roosevelt, Lincoln and Nixon. ... But I don't like Bush who always destroys other countries' sovereignty and is a double-faced man." Several other students also referred to Bush as a double-faced man and resented the role of America as the world's policeman. Still, one student wasn't disturbed by "hardball" politics. "American statesmen also exert a strong influence on the turn of world affairs. Like George W. Bush—he is quite a hardball who may irritate others with some of his policies. Anyway, I think America is a strong power and would like everyone else to see it clearly, too. I also think it's not too bad a thing. Anyway, the world needs a strong head to lead it out of the mess and to be happy."

Last, "I admire the former USA President—Bill Clinton—very much, and I just find that Mr. Bush is only something like a president, who was not a top student at Yale University."

So, this is what China's young people think about the United States—admiration for its strengths but dissatisfaction with how the country uses its strength. In addressing these statements to my class, I simply told them they could find voices in America that agreed with them and that controversy is part of our system.

CREATURE DISCOMFORTS

So far this semester, the creature count in my apartment has included one rat, one cockroach, five mosquitoes, and four mini-moths. The last are dark brown, resemble moths, and measure about a quarter of an inch. Unlike the mosquitoes, they are harmless. As for the rat, it has been taken care of, and as I noted to my fellow teachers and Yang Yan, it was nothing like the gigantic rats I had seen crawling out of gutters in Manhattan. Chinese rats were much smaller than American rats. That, said Yang Yan with a straight face, is because China is a developing country. Still, when it comes to cockroaches, Chinese cockroaches win hands down. The New York City roach seems delicate by comparison.

I don't know why I am always amazed at how the Chinese conduct business here, but I am. Even if I were a professional mind reader, I would still have to cope with trying to read the mind in Chinese. Even then, I would face one of those cultural subtleties that require years of learning. My favorite example of how much I have to learn occurred one drizzly morning when a student was to meet me at my apartment. She was taking me to meet some of her family. She arrived with an umbrella in hand, and I put on a rain jacket. As we were leaving, she nodded toward my umbrella and asked me if I wanted to take it. "No," I said, "it's not raining hard; my jacket is enough."

"Are you sure you don't want to take your umbrella?"

I was sure. We started down the stairs—five double flights of them. As we walked, she said we would go to the number twenty-five bus terminal. I said that was fine because we were more likely to get a seat on the bus. We continued downstairs. As we approached the bottom, she informed me that she had to return the umbrella she was carrying to one of the shop owners; she had borrowed it when she had gotten off the bus, as it was raining heavily then. "You mean, you needed my umbrella?" I said. "Why didn't you tell me when we were upstairs?"

"You are angry," she said.

"No," I answered, "but I am not happy. That is a lot of stairs. Why didn't you ask me for my umbrella?"

"If you were Chinese," she said, "you would know I needed your umbrella."

There are countless experiences like the above. "Why didn't you come to the performance last night?" someone will ask us foreign teachers. We didn't come because no one told us about the performance. A class doesn't show up: "Oh, the department is taking them on a trip." No one told us. "You must submit your course lesson plans." This, eight weeks into a semester. Is all this frustrating? Sometimes infuriating? Yes, but such events are also funny, and they make good stories to laugh about over dinner. And we foreign experts must keep our Chinese counterparts laughing over their dinners as well.

My latest lesson in subtlety began with one of those typical Chinese phone calls. One of my former faculty students asked if I could meet with her husband and his business friends. On my previous stay here, I had spent such a day with her husband and his friend so they could practice their English. That was fine with me. I was told a car would come for me at 8:00 a.m. on Sunday. That's when I discovered I was being invited to a company to meet with several of their personnel. As usual, I had no idea what I was to do. No book, no topic of discussion, no idea how large the group was or how long I was expected to meet, what the format for the meeting was, or anything more than a car was coming for me at 8 a.m.

I was taken to Changzhou's New District, an area of new enterprises and luxury apartments. There, I was taken to a conference room and in short order met about fifteen businesspeople and their English teacher. I was to spend the next two hours talking to them and making them talk to me in English. These salespeople and workers spend their Sunday mornings learning English and, like me, have worked a regular week and gotten up at six or so in the morning to participate in the class. The lesson went well, and I guess I am pleased to know I can still pull rabbits from a hat if necessary. After two hours, I was taken around the New District apartment complex, which is nothing short of magnificent. Rents in one of the small apartments, I was told, begin at four thousand yuan a month. That is about $500 in United States currency. A good deal for an American but very pricey for a Chinese worker, whose salary of one to two thousand yuan a month is considered a living wage.

Over lunch, I found the purpose of the morning was to decide whether the company wanted to make me an offer to teach every Sunday morning. The class I had talked with was a way to see if they liked me and thought I was any good. If I did not meet their expectations, they would simply have thanked me for coming that day, fed me well, and sent me home. I would have had a pleasant morning and a wonderful lunch, and my feelings would have been spared. On the other hand, if I had known that the morning's lesson was a kind of trial and then not have been offered anything, I would have lost face. So, if things seem mysterious here, it is more likely a way of being polite. I hope to continue learning this way of doing things, but I could do without the creatures.

SOME PROGRESS IN MY CHINESE

I am feeling uncommonly proud of myself these days. I had bought a battery for my camera only to find it was as dead as the one it was supposed to replace. Of course, I did not have anything like a sales slip, so I had to hope the salesperson remembered my face. The battery cost twenty-eight yuan, a princely sum here, equivalent to $3.50, or more than a week's lunches. Then, there was negotiating a replacement in Chinese. Well, the saleswoman did remember me and my very primitive Chinese worked. I received another battery free of charge. This was followed by another small triumph. In the market, where I went to buy a breadstick, I handed the vendor a two-jiao note (there are ten jiao to a yuan). He shook his head and held up four fingers. "No, two," I said in English, holding up two fingers. "Two," someone echoed. Everyone, including the vendor, laughed. The price of a breadstick is two jiao, and he was simply trying to take advantage of a foreigner.

I also filled out the forms for a Times card. Please consider that this was all done in Chinese. The Times is a local Western-style supermarket and, like the supermarkets at home, offers privileges for cardholders. I am supposed to receive all kinds of special deals as a cardholder, but so far, I have not seen any discounts when my bill is rung up. I am certain, however, that even if I spend an astronomical amount these months, I won't be awarded a Thanksgiving turkey.

I can't tell you how pleased I am with my progress here as I learn more and more characters and expressions. My tones, however, have not improved, but generally I am understood. I also feel more confident making my way around China—so long as exchanges remain simple.

This year at the college I have noticed a great change in the student body. There are, first of all, about three thousand more students here than before, for a total student population of eight thousand. The character of the students has also changed. In my first year here, if a boy and girl were walking hand in hand, they would immediately drop hands and move slightly apart if anyone else appeared who could see them. Now I see many couples, not only holding hands but also with the boy's arm around the girl or a girl clinging to a boy's arm, all very open. In some of the less populated areas of the college, some couples are in tight embraces. Having a boyfriend or girlfriend seems to be a priority for students these days. Couples pair off earlier than before as well. I also have noticed a change in attitude. My students are still polite to me, but in almost all other ways, they remind me of American students—rather disinterested in their studies and eager for parties and friends. The local internet café's are packed with boys playing computer games, and when I have awakened in the middle of the night, I can see from my window the lights of computer screens still on at the cafés. It costs about two yuan an hour at an internet café, so these students have pocket money to spare. I go to the cafés for my email early in the morning, when few students are present—not only to ensure having a computer at my disposal but also to avoid the cigarette smoke. Chinese men and boys smoke heavily.

This semester, I have caught four students copying each other's work and in two cases plagiarizing. I have told all my classes now that if this happens again, the students who copy will be dismissed from my class. Apart from the occasional copying, which is also attempted by students at home, student excuses here are pretty typical. "I forgot my work in the dorm" or "I lost my paper" are typical. I usually tell my students that if they can think up a really creative excuse that I haven't heard before, I shall give them credit. I do like the excuse one student sent my colleague, apologizing for his absence. "I was suffering from 'allergic rhinitis.'" We think that means hay fever.

A CHANGZOU THANKSGIVING

Thanksgiving is strictly an American holiday, so of course the Chinese do not celebrate it. Several restaurants here claim to serve Western food and offer what they claim is a Thanksgiving Day dinner. Their menus offered little of what is traditional, so my fellow foreign experts and I decided to settle on a good Chinese dinner.

The restaurant we chose offers foods from several areas in China. Everything, from soups to nuts, is on display. A waiter followed us around as we made our selections, each of us picking something we thought we would like to eat. By the time we had finished ordering dishes for the main courses, our appetizers were waiting for us at our table. Here is our Changzhou Thanksgiving menu:

For appetizers, we chose five dishes. These included thin slices of marinated pork kidney; a creamy tofu sprinkled with green onion, spicy bread crumbs, and thousand-year egg; shredded celery and bamboo shoots; and lotus. This last, when sliced, resembles tomato, but is sweetened and firmer than tomato. Pickled beans, peanuts, and a small dish of fried noodles similar to what is served in Chinese restaurants at home were compliments of the house.

Our main courses included sweet-and-sour fish with tofu, orange chicken, roast goose with potatoes in a broth; goat meat; greens and a variety of steamed mushrooms with bamboo shoots, and an Indian bread. The last is a very thin flat bread and quite tasty. The house supplied pumpkin cakes, small rounds of pumpkin filled with bean paste and quite sweet, and watermelon wedges.

We congratulated ourselves on our selection of restaurant and menu, and since we all liked the roast goose, and since roast goose is a Christmas type of fare, we decided we may do our Christmas dinner at this place as well. The cost of this feast for all six of us was the equivalent of thirty American dollars.

So, Thanksgiving here left us stuffed and groaning, and we had warm company. What we all missed, however, was the company of family and friends.

A STORY OF THE CHINESE ZODIAC

The Chinese follow a lunar calendar, so this year, February first marks the beginning of the new year. This year is the year of the goat, and what follows is a story of the Chinese zodiac by one of my English writing students. If it seems to be told too simply for you, it is because the assignment was to tell a traditional Chinese story for an eight-to-ten-year-old English-speaking child. (This is one way to teach how an audience changes the language and sentence structure of what a writer writes.)

Twelve Zodiacal Animals

Have you ever heard of the twelve Zodiacal animals in China? What kinds of twelve animals you might ask. They're the rat, buffalo, tiger, rabbit, dragon, snake, horse, goat, monkey, rooster, dog and pig in proper order. Each year has a sign of animal. It is quite different with the Western twelve Zodiacal signs. Take me, for example. I was born the 17th of September, 1981. The sign of 1981 is the rooster in China, and the 17th of September is Virgo in Western Countries.

Maybe you will think that there are so many animals in the world, why did the Chinese people choose these twelve animals. Here is a funny myth; it will satisfy your curiosity.

It is said that the king of paradise suddenly announced a command. There would be held a race-match for every animal and the first twelve animals would be picked as the sign of a year. In other words, twelve animals which ran faster than any other animals would enjoy the honor. The competition was very intense, but to everyone's surprise the rat came first. Why? It was so small and weak.

As a matter of fact, the rat climbed on the buffalo's back and hid himself very well. Nobody observed. When the buffalo approached the finish line, he was sure that he must be the champion, but he counted his chickens before they were hatched. The rat used him as a gangplank, jumped over the finish line and of course won the first prize. The rat is cunning, but I want to say it is very clever.

And do you know why the cat is absent in this game? She runs faster than the pig at least. As we know the dog is a natural enemy of the cat. But, in ancient times, they were friends. They both planned to take part in the match. Cat's duty is to catch mice during the night. She must make good use of the time before the match to sleep. Then she can compete full of vigor. So she asked the dog to wake her. Dog promised on the surface, but was toying with the idea of how to reduce his adversaries. So he sold cat down the river. He didn't wake cat. Cat didn't awaken until the dog returned with flying colors because dog had won the eleventh prize. Cat broke ties with dog and began to hate dog's guts. Now you see that's the reason why cats hate dogs so much. You can't suppose that dog was so deceitful. No wonder that when cat meets dog, her cute features change.

Have you found that there's only one animal you can't find in practical life? Yes, that's the dragon. It's illusory and based on imagination. It's also the totem and symbol of China. You cannot but admire the Chinese people's creativity and imagination.

Okay, tell me which year you were born and then I'll tell you which animal is your sign.

Unfortunately, my student did not put her name on this paper, but when I track down who she is, I'll give her proper credit for this very charming folktale.

CHINESE NEW YEAR STORY AND OTHER ODDS AND ENDS

Based on the lunar calendar, Chinese New Year will begin on February 1 this year. During the two to six weeks of the festival, most families will get together, and this means all of China is on the move—on buses, trains, and planes—to see their relatives. The time is spent in feasting. For children, the holiday means gifts of money from parents and relatives and new clothes. Doors are decorated with characters representing wishes for, among them, good fortune, health, and longevity. And, of course, there are fireworks. This last part of the celebration comes with a story.

A long, long time ago, there was a ferocious monster named Nian. Once a year, in the dark of the night, he came out of the forest into the village, where he ate all the villagers' livestock. Sometimes, he even ate the villagers. Everyone feared Nian. At the time of year when he was expected to come, the villagers huddled together in the village square, lighting fires to keep warm. One year, just before Nian was expected to arrive, a villager threw some bamboo pieces into the fire. These exploded with a loud noise, and Nian was frightened away. Now, every new year, there are fireworks to keep Nian away. He no longer bothers people. All that is left of him is his name, which is also the Chinese word for "year."

One afternoon in class, I heard the sound of a band. Looking out the window, I saw what I assumed was a parade. My students giggled when I asked if the day was a festival of some sorts. No, it was a funeral. Now, traditional mourning clothes are white, and the students told me the coffin, too, would be draped in white. What I saw, however, was a coffin draped in red, the color of happiness. Perhaps, I suggested to the class, this was a rich uncle who died, and all the relatives were happy because they would inherit a lot of money. I later asked Yang Yan why the coffin was draped in red rather than white and learned that a red coffin meant the person had led a long life and would soon be joining his or her ancestors in heaven. This was to be celebrated. White, on the other hand, is usually for children.

I have mentioned the building and road work being done here in Changzhou, but I haven't mentioned the trees. Trees and gardens are springing up everywhere. Along the recently widened road near our school, the entire road is being planted with trees along its sides. Parks and greenery are sprouting up all over town, a refreshing and welcome sight. The trees are also a part of a new program to plant trees throughout China. In the northwest of China, the desert is growing rapidly. In addition to destroying farmland, the sand causes terrible sandstorms, some of which blanket Beijing. By planting trees in the northwest and major cities, the Chinese hope to prevent the further loss of farmland

and alleviate the effects of pollution. The soft coal burned here in factories and residences north of the Yangzi fills the air with soot. In Beijing, one seldom sees the stars or moon at night and respiratory diseases are common. Trees should help.

A last bit of news. Yang Yan has found me a calligraphy teacher, and what a teacher! Hong Xisheng is an internationally known calligrapher and artist. We meet every Tuesday afternoon for two hours, and I am learning to write my Chinese name in running script, a series of graceful curves and loops. I am also picking up the words for the four treasures of calligraphy: ink stick, ink stone, paper, and brushes. Thanks to Mr. Hong, I now have excellent brushes and good ink, which make writing characters a good deal easier. While I am here, he will teach me two characters: longevity and happiness. These traditional characters grace Chinese doors for Spring Festival, the holiday that marks the beginning of the new year.

CHINESE SPAGHETTI AND OTHER GOOD MEALS

Michelle, Julia and Phil Smith, and I often share our dinners together in the kitchen shared by the foreign experts. We all chip in for the food, and Julia does the honors with the wok. Dinners vary. Phil Smith likes meat and for one dinner made us all a beef stew. This meant tracking down some beef, not generally at the markets, as chicken and pork are the common meats here. It was an excellent stew, and Phil persuaded Yang Yan to try some. Stew is not typical Chinese fare, so we were pleased to see that Yang Yan found it very tasty and not too bad at all for Western food. My contribution was roast duck from the little market and then what I can only describe as Chinese spaghetti. The easy part was the canned tomatoes. Perhaps a trip to Beijing markets would have permitted me some olive oil and basil, but Changzhou had only canned tomatoes to offer. No tomato paste. No onions anywhere. The sauce, therefore, lacked a certain oomph. The real challenge was finding spaghetti. I looked at every kind of noodles the Times supermarket had to offer but saw nothing like the spaghetti at home. South of the Yangzi, rice is the main crop; north of the river is wheat country. The closest I came to spaghetti was a package of rice noodles. So, there you have it: Chinese spaghetti, not a total failure but nothing like home.

The four of us also have tried a few restaurants, one of them the recently opened Pizza Hut and a favorite of Chinese students. We found it overpriced and not too bad but not the pizza we preferred at home. The best deal for the yuan is a Muslim restaurant in the center of Changzhou's shopping district. Its main offering is lamb and lots of it. Truly the best lamb I have ever eaten. Another memorable offering was the dessert of sugared apples. For me, on a daily basis, I patronize a dumpling restaurant across the street from the college's back gate. Right inside the entrance, I watched two women prepare the dumpling dough, which looks like a simple mix of flour and water rolled into a long fat-noodle shape. From this, small pieces are broken off to hold the filling. The filling could be anything from pork and chicken to vegetables and red bean paste. Guan Chunying made me a small card with the Chinese characters for the various fillings and their English meanings. The Chinese word for "dumpling" is "jiaozi," and the "skin," or dough that holds the filling, is "pi." What made this dumpling place especially good was that the skin was light; most other dumpling skins, similar to what is served in Chinese restaurants at home, are a bit heavier and "doughy."

New to us in the foreign affairs office is Professor Chen, a visiting professor from Taiwan. He is at the college to help faculty prepare research grants. Such grants are important for both the college and the faculty member. Mr. Chen was delightful; he had spent many years in the United States and not only was fluent in English but was also familiar with American humor. I enjoyed talking with him and discovered that his work in Changzhou was not unusual: there were many such collaborations between Taiwan and mainland China. He predicted that one day Taiwan would peacefully become part of the People's Republic of China. We invited him to join us one evening for dinner at the Muslim restaurant.

MY CALLIGRAPHY MASTER

My favorite Chinese words for ten weeks now are "dui," "hao," and "haode," said to me by Mr. Hong, my calligraphy master. The words mean "correct," "good," and "okay." The okay meant I had done a whole character well, and if the character also had beauty, "haode" was followed by an exuberant "okay!" and a thumbs-up. "Okay" was one of three English words that Mr. Hong knew—the other two were "hello" and "goodbye."

I mentioned that Mr. Hong has an international reputation as a calligrapher, and when we first met, he presented me with a book of his work and inscribed it to me. I found that he had also given the same book to Jiang Zemin.

Calligraphy has its ceremonies. Before I begin to write, I must first wet the ink stone. The ink stone resembles a small dish and has a lid. I wash both of these in cool water, leaving a little water on each. Next, I spread some newspaper on a table; this will absorb any excess ink that seeps through the exercise sheets. On top of the newspaper, I place a sheet of exercise paper and hold it in place with two weights. The weights are specially designed for this purpose. They measure about eight inches in length and two in width and are just heavy enough to keep the exercise paper firmly in place. The exercise paper consists of twelve squares;

each square is bisected horizontally, then vertically, and then diagonally left to right and right to left. These lines help the beginning calligrapher write a character in the correct proportions. Once all this is set up, I wet my brush, squeezing any excess moisture into the ink stone dish. Then I shake the bottle of ink and pour a small amount into the ink dish. I mix the water and ink with my brush and use the ink stone lid to wipe of the excess ink as well as to form a fine point on the end of the brush. Now, I am ready to work.

I learned one character at a time. I began with a four-stroke character followed by an eight-stroke character. This character had all the eight basic strokes used in calligraphy, and forming them in the proper way takes both patience and practice. As a beginner, I must learn not only to put the proper pressure on the brush but also how to make a character in perfect proportion. Before I left Changzhou, I worked on both traditional and cursive forms of Chinese writing, aiming for the cursive form of "shou," the Chinese character for "longevity."

In addition to learning how to write Chinese characters, I have learned much of the vocabulary. Each of the eight Chinese strokes that compose a character has a name. The "dot" that often makes up a part of a character also has many names; these describe the form of the dot, such as "tiger's claw." My vocabulary doesn't include the variations.

Once I have done my practicing, there is a closing "ceremony." The ink stone and brushes must be cleaned, the brush tip made into a perfect form and the brush hung to dry. Generally, I also set up for my next day of practice.

Mr. Hong's goal for me was the cursive form of "shou." I did well with that, so he also taught me the cursive forms of "fu" and "lu." The former means "happiness" and the latter "good wishes." He also pronounced me a calligrapher. I had joked with him at our first meeting that I would be lucky to charge fifty cents for one of my characters, as opposed to the $1,250 he receives for one character. At the end of our lessons, he said I could charge ten yuan at least—about a dollar twenty-five. Actually, I am now better than that.

THE FOUR TREASURES OF CALLIGRAPHY

The photograph below shows the four treasures of Chinese art and calligraphy: ink stone, ink stick, brush, and paper. Most practitioners of Chinese calligraphy use prepared ink, but for an artist, the ink stick is indispensable, as it enables the artist to adjust the depth of color in his work. Depending on the amount of ink and water in the ink stone, the artist can draw deep black outlines or pale shades of gray. Much of early Chinese art is black on white, and even today, simple black-and-white paintings are regarded as superior to later works, which use color. It's a bit like film buffs who prefer the early black-and-white films to the modern Technicolor offerings

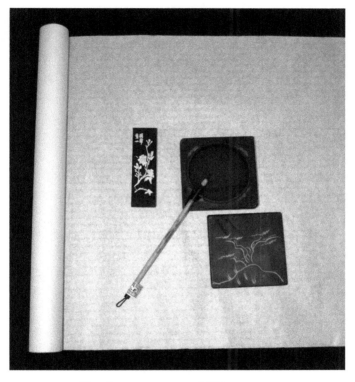

The four treasures of Chinese art:
paper, brush, ink stick and ink stone.

The brush shown in the photograph is the one I use to do small characters; these are approximately an inch high. There are both smaller and larger characters, and brushes vary in size according to the size of the character. I have worked in several sizes, and my brushes range in size from the small one shown in the photograph to one the size of the tail on a white tail deer. The hair of the brush comes from rabbit, goat, or wolf, though I doubt many wolf-hair brushes exist today.

Chinese characters also vary in form; the earliest form is now called "seal" style. It developed from ancient Chinese characters carved on bones; the bones were used to divine fortunes and predict the future. Seal script is often called bone script. It is used on chops, the seals people use to sign their names. Each chop is unique to the person, carrying his or her name. A seal generally appears at the end of a poem or work of art. The other forms of Chinese writing include traditional, official, and cursive. There is also a "running" style, in which characters run into each other, forming a string of "words." Most of these cannot be read; they are expressions of the calligrapher's character and are not really meant to be read; it's a bit like the varying brush strokes one sees in Western paintings—think of the difference among the works of Van Gogh, Cezanne, and Jackson Pollock.

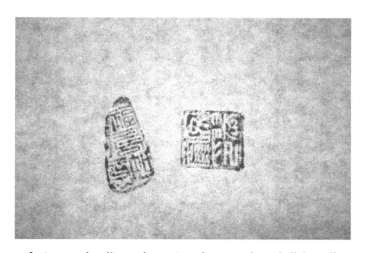

Artists and calligraphers sign their work with "chops". The red square shown here is my Chinese name in ancient characters and it is as unique to me as my fingerprints. The other seal is a decorative one; some artists have several such seals.

Here, I have included a sample of my work; it comes from a line of Mao's poetry and translates as "The very clouds foam above white cloud mountain." The characters are traditional. I have also worked on cursive characters. Each of these styles required a different frame of mind. Cursive characters have a rhythm and are done in one elaborate stroke, whereas traditional characters demand patience and care. Each of the characters in the line of Mao's poetry uses one or more of the eight basic strokes of Chinese writing.

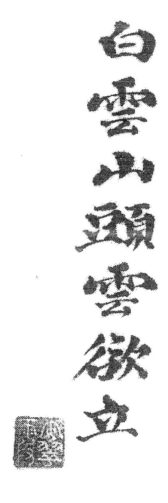

At the end of the line of poetry and to the left, I have put my seal. This is my Chinese name done in "seal" style. I have also included (above) two seals—one a larger version of my name and the second a decorative seal. Chinese art, which generally includes calligraphy—often a poem—carries several seals. Seals can be easily distinguished as they are done in red ink. There may be two or more of the artist's names. Many poets and artists took on, or were given, other descriptive names. The decorative seals add a pleasant meaning to the work. I am not sure what my decorative seal means. It was given to me by Mr. Hong, my calligraphy teacher, who spoke only a few words of English.

ANOTHER CLASSROOM ADVENTURE

After explaining the class systems in England and the United States to my American/British culture classes, I asked my students. "And what is the class system in China?" There were big smiles and a few laughs but no response. "Don't you know?" I asked.

Finally: "There are no classes in a Marxist country."

"Of course," I said. "That means everyone in China is the same."

"Nooo," came a small chorus of voices.

China has farmers (about 70 per cent of the population) and a very wealthy, though small, business class. The students saw themselves somewhere in the middle, so I suggested there were three classes in China. Actually, a sociologist would make some finer distinctions, because being a party member carries its own special weight here. An economist would recognize the beginnings of capitalism, though the word has been sanitized as a "free enterprise system" or a "market economy." Although students often cite the ideological response to questions, the inequities and injustices here come through in other ways. For instance, one student wrote a composition about the college entrance exams. These are very competitive; trying for a place in Beijing or Qinghua universities is akin to trying to get into Harvard or Yale. My student writer reported that all the top students in her class failed to enter top schools, but to everyone's surprise, several of the poorer but still wealthy students had gotten places in such universities. She later learned that one of her classmate's fathers had contributed a million yuan to that university.

This student's school catered to the children of well-to-do and very wealthy families. There is such a school in Changzhou. Students at these schools do not study as diligently as most Chinese students do because they know their parents can buy their way into colleges and good business positions. I am happy that most of my students are first-generation college students whose parents have sacrificed to give them an education. Upper middle school in China—equivalent to grades ten through twelve in the States—isn't free. Economics forces many young people to stop their education at the end of middle school. Although the schools are supposed to be equal in what they offer, they are not, and Chinese students or their parents all talk about getting into the "best school" in their city. Some places, however, are reserved for "top" students: scoring above 620 on a 650-point series of tests will provide a student a free ride through senior middle school.

Parents actively support their children's efforts throughout the school years. My students have written many papers telling how they were lazy students or how they had difficulty with a particular subject and how they changed to become top students in their class. Seldom do students blame a teacher or claim they "can't do" a subject. They take responsibility for their own performance, good or bad. "Where there's a will, there's a way" is a favorite saying here. Another is "failure is the mother of success," often told a child who has done poorly in a subject. Trying harder, studying more, practicing more, and asking for help until they conquer the subject are the answers to a poor or middling performance. It stands in sharp contrast to the attitudes of many American children, who often feel that they lack a "gift" for a subject. The poor part of the education system here is the total reliance on tests. Excellent students with outstanding records can crumble before some of these examinations. I have also found it difficult this year trying to teach my English composition classes different ways to write, as there is only one way required on tests of English mastery. Chinese students do think for themselves but not for their studies. They know what pays off in a subject: successfully passing the national test in the subject. One of my students is committing to memory ten thousand (yes, that is ten thousand) English words in order to pass the level eight mastery test in English. I doubt that most Americans know that many English words.

A VISIT WITH YANG YAN'S PARENTS

This weekend I am off to Nanjing with Yang Yan to meet her parents. She once told me that first year when we became friends that her first seven years of life were spent with her grandmother and that she fought going to her parents when they were able to be a family. Yan claimed to have little feeling for her mother, yet in the time I knew Yan, she was a very caring and dutiful daughter. Having left a tearful toddler off at a preschool, I knew how difficult it must have been for her mother to give over the care of her child, even if it was to her own mother. Hong Yun, as Yang Yan's mother was named, had been a dancer in a Red Army troupe that traveled throughout China performing at army bases and in farming communities. I was curious about her life, both as a dancer and a soldier. It was at our meeting that I most regretted my inability to speak Chinese, particularly when she said through Yang Yan how good it was to speak to someone her own age.

Yang Yan, me, Hong Yun

Yang Yan's father, mother and me at lunch;
note the many dishes, typical of Chinese meals.

Hong Yun was born in 1935. At age fourteen, she joined the Red Army as part of a performing art troupe. Her brother and sister had already joined the army, and an uncle who saw her perform in a local propaganda group encouraged her also to join the army. He felt she would have a good future performing for the farmers and others. The group focused on folk tunes and stories. In the army, she both sang and danced; she was also trained in both arts.

In 1956, with the Great Leap Forward, she was sent to a smaller city. Since her family had been fairly prosperous, she was not considered "Red" enough and had no powerful Communist Party member to sponsor her, ending both her acting career and her singing career. She was now simply part of a dance troupe. Here, she met her husband, also a part of the Red Army. A good part of their early marriage life found them often apart in different cities. When she gave birth to first Yang Yan and then a younger daughter, her leave was for forty days only. Their children were raised by their grandmother, Yang Yan for the first seven years of her life.

A talented dancer who made famous her performance and interpretation of her lotus dance, she evidently aroused jealousy and resentment among her colleagues. She also felt she was too outspoken and assertive. Most of what she would have liked to do with her career as a performer was denied her. She was sent instead to teach dance to children.

"We were the sacrificial generation," she said. Younger generations had different goals and ambitions and didn't understand the period she and their parents lived through—the Cultural Revolution—enamored by the ideals of Communism and its reforms. Later, she saw these ideals become dust.

Now retired, she was given an apartment and, I gather, a pension. Still a beautiful woman, she, at sixty-seven, is extremely trim and limber. When she talks, her hands move with a dancer's grace. She demonstrated a dance step from the province where Mao Zedong was from, a very common folk-dance step and danced everywhere. Today, the step is modified and basically used as part of dance exercise, as I do in the square with Xu Ping.

Hong Yun is mentioned in several dance encyclopedia and has also written about dance. She said she would like to have been a designer and had designed her own costumes.

A FEW WRINKLES IN LIFE

I came home from class one afternoon to find that a security alarm had been installed in my apartment. A small white box with a large red button had been placed next to my bed. In case of an emergency—what sort was unspecified—I needed only to press the button and the police would come. Somehow, that button made me as well as my fellow foreign experts feel suddenly insecure. Three of us had lived quite safely here for more than half a year without such an emergency button, and all of us had been living here for several months without the button. This being China, we all felt that some poor foreign expert had been done in, and the local police had decided this was the way to ensure our safety.

This little wrinkle in my life passed quickly, and my only fear was that one day I may bump the button somehow, and the entire Changzhou police force would be breaking down my door. As a matter of fact. I did think I might have to call the police to break down my door. One morning as I went to leave my rooms, the door would not open. I found myself locked in my apartment and no amount of jiggling, tugging, or swearing would open my door. I made a desperate call to Yang Yan and after several times of telling her, no, I did not forget my keys (happens now and then); no, I wasn't locked out of my apartment. I was locked IN and could not get OUT; and no, the guesthouse maintenance man wasn't around that day. She said she would come over. "Perhaps I should press the red button," I said. I might as well have said I was pressing the button to begin WW III. I was rescued by Yang Yan and Peter, one of my fellow teachers here. We made a mess of the door—the entire doorknob had to be removed—but I was freed. Still, I wonder what that red button is for.

Since I have started my calligraphy lessons, my week's work has settled into a pattern of classes on Monday through Thursday; correcting papers all week; calligraphy lesson on Tuesday afternoons; Ping-Pong on Wednesday afternoons; and practicing calligraphy for at least an hour and a half to two hours a day. I began with one four-stroke character, graduated to an eight-stroke character, and am now working on the sixteen-stroke character for "longevity." I am learning to do this character in its ancient form and over the weekend. I shall work my way up to its simplified, modern version. There are three separate forms—all of them traditional—for the longevity character, and I must master these before I can begin the cursive version of the word. I discovered that whereas I could do three sheets of an eight-stroke word (that is, write it thirty-six times) in two hours, I can do only two sheets of a sixteen-stroke character (that is, write it twenty-four times) in that same period of time. Mr. Hong, my calligraphy master, knows all the forms—from seal style (or ancient bone script) and official style to cursive and running script. In one of his characters, he has used all the styles to form one character. This requires a mastery not only of the brush but also of the many turns and styles of Chinese characters. Here I am struggling with just one—I shall be, according to Yang Yan—a "one-character calligraphy master." Believe it or not, this is a worthy title.

"Shou," the Chinese character for "longevity" has eight hundred variations, one hundred in ancient seal style. It is one of the eight forms Mr. Hong taught me: four traditional and four cursive. This "shou" is cursive.

This cursive form of shou is done in one long brush stroke. Other cursive forms are more abstract and make lovely works of art. They are even more difficult to master.

"Fu," the character for "happiness," hangs on most Chinese doors. It is often hung upside down, as this upside-down form resembles the character for "to come in." So, the meaning invites happiness to come into the home. This is also the cursive form, but I had to work on the traditional form first.

Though the character fu looks fairly simple, it took many hours of practice to master. It involved two strokes, an easy one on the left and a tricky one on the right as the correct shape and exact spacing were a constant challenge. I did enjoy forming the looping curve as the end.

"Lu," which invites good wishes to come in, always looked like a dragon to me. Using a large brush for the characters, I enjoyed the sweep of the character's "tail."

Lu was my reward for being a diligent student. Mr. Hong's plan was to teach me just two characters but added lu when he recognized I was willing to practice. It is traditional to wish both good health and good fortune to a wish for a long life.

The Chinese characters on the left of my work are my signature for my Chinese name, done in running style. Below my signature is the seal bearing my name in ancient bone style. This form was most difficult of all to master.

Mr. Hong and I pose before my rendition of happiness. Despite his lack of English and my minimal Chinese, we got along famously and had a lot of fun.

HOMEWARD BOUND

When I start dreaming of hamburgers, I know it's time to come home. I generally don't eat hamburgers, but this past week, the yearning became such a longing that I hit the Changzhou McDonald's. I can now vouch for the fact that the food is just the same terrible food that McDonald's serves at home. It is expensive by Chinese standards but a bit cheaper than the food at home. The day I went for lunch, I was the only foreigner in the place, and I felt I was giving the local branch a sense of authenticity. One big difference here is that the young women who staff the place not only bus the tables but wait on them as well. Is that upscale or not?

My first year in Changzhou, I ate as much of the duck as can be eaten—head, foot, tongue, blood, and everything in-between. This year, the challenge has been the pig—liver, lung, stomach, brains, throat, and intestines besides the regular meat. Chinese pigs are sweeter than those at home, so many of the parts that have too strong a taste for the American palate are quite delicious here.

My first year in Changzhou, I had bronchitis, and this year I had a return bout. The weather here has been bone-chilling cold, and classrooms, offices, houses, and restaurants are not heated. The theory seems to be that south of the Yangzi, there is no need for heat. Although my apartment is heated, the heater failed to work properly during a week of cold and rain that marked the beginning of January. My heating unit froze up. My quest to stay warm involved parboiling myself in the bathtub in the evening and getting under the covers as quickly as possible. In the mornings, after dressing in a flash, I filled several buckets of boiling water to pour over the ice-encrusted heating unit outside my window. This needed to be repeated several times a day in order for me to have any heat in my room. Now, the days have turned sunny; the unit has defrosted, and I am toasty warm once more. I still have a cough that would make me a natural for the closing acts in *La Bohème* and *La Traviata*, but I feel good. All of us foreign experts sniffle, sneeze, and cough.

Another repeat of my first year in Changzhou is calligraphy. This year, however, I am taught by a master, and he has pronounced me a calligrapher. I find the study of Chinese and Chinese characters endlessly fascinating, so I shall probably be boring people to tears when I return home.

A POSTSCRIPT OF SORTS

My friends in China have been updating me on SARS, the abbreviation for severe acute respiratory syndrome, a flulike virus that can lead to death and was rampant through China. Believed to be caused by birds—chicken, ducks, and geese—SARS became a major health threat in mid-2003, a few months after I had returned home. The flu is highly contagious and spreads easily, as it is airborne. Thousands of chickens and other poultry were destroyed, travel was curtailed, and several areas were quarantined. Michelle Day, the English girl who taught with me at the college, emailed what had been happening at the college.

"So, just when things started to be falling into place, the SARS outbreak began to take hold in China. It has been so strange, because I have known about this since December, but I kept talking about it to people in China and nobody seemed to know anything. Even up until about three weeks ago nobody seems to realize the seriousness of it. Things have completely changed now though. I am in a province which only has four cases, but nobody here is taking any chances. For the last two weeks, every single place you can think of has been disinfected. My room is sprayed constantly and classrooms always smell of vinegar which is not exactly a nice smell. Nobody in my city (Changzhou) is allowed to go outside of this city, so I cannot travel anywhere on the weekends. My one week holiday has been cancelled also, and I have to work as normal with no rest. The worst of it is that the university campus has been turned into a prison. The students are not allowed to leave the campus at any time. The gates have been locked and they are unable to get out. This is so boring for them because they have no TV and all the social activities on this small campus have been cancelled because the Changzhou government have banned large social events taking place in the city. The students must eat, sleep, drink and do everything within this 'prison' (as they call it). All this, and not one case of SARS has been discovered in Changzhou.

"I am not as affected as the students because I can go out, but I am advised not to. The safety of the foreigners is taken so seriously."

One of the students has emailed me the following about life on the campus:

"Sorry again. Our school has closed. No one can go out without permission card except the teachers. The students who want to play computer games just can play them in the small internet café under the number 9 dorm building in our school. So it is hard for me to find a computer to send you an email. I tried three times. This time is lucky. The situation is more serious in Jiangsu now. SARS has broken out in NaiJing, and ZhengJiang (the city near Changzhou) has found a case. And my home city has found cases, too. It's a hard time. No one knows how it will be. It seems that every generation has a crisis period in history. My grandfather met the war. My father met the Cultural Revolution which has changed the fate of many Chinese people, including my father. Now I meet SARS, a virus we know what it is but haven't learned to how to conquer it, just can passively accept it. I am not worrying about it too much. God will choose who to leave, who stay."

Although Michelle's email noted four cases in Jiangsu province, a more recent email from a faculty friend reports that there are now fourteen cases. Television now reports the cases, a significant change from the secretiveness of the past.

HOW THE GOVERNMENT
HANDLED THE CRISIS

My friend from my first year in China, Nell Warnes, emailed me another account of the SARS epidemic; it provides insight into how officialdom handles some things.

Although this is long, I hope you will find it interesting. I think my dates are fairly accurate, but I did not record the earlier ones at the time. I have searched the internet for the dates the WHO (World Health Organization) team went to Beijing and the Amoy Garden apartments were quarantined in Hong Kong, but I wasn't able to find them. If someone knows, please let me know. Please give me some feedback. I am concerned about whether this will get through.

Around the middle of March, I went for my usual weekly lesson with Mrs. Yu, our contact with the college and the assistant to the foreign affairs officer (who is apparently too busy to take care of us personally; also, he speaks less English than Mrs. Yu). I give her an hour of English conversation practice every week on Tuesday afternoons. I asked Mrs. Yu if she had heard of SARS. She hadn't. So I told her what the acronym stands for. She looked up "acute" and "respiratory" in her dictionary.

"Oh, a typical pneumonia. Are you worried about this?" she asked.

"Yes, I am concerned," I said.

"Don't worry about this." She laughed. "There were a few cases in Guangzhou, but the government has this under control now. We haven't heard anything about this on the news."

"I know," I said quietly, "but Mrs. Yu, did you know there is a team of doctors from the World Health Organization in Beijing right now?"

She looked at me, her eyes widening. "Oh!" she exclaimed. "So serious?"

"Yes," I replied.

"I will check to see if this is true," she said matter-of-factly.

"Can you get the internet on this computer?" I countered. She nodded. I took her to the WHO website.

"Don't worry about this," she repeated. "I am sure it is not so serious, or we would have heard about it on the news…"

A couple of weeks later, the internet news was full of the hundreds of cases in Hong Kong and the quarantine of an apartment complex. Still there was nothing about SARS on the Chinese TV news or in the newspapers.

"Mrs. Yu," I said, "what about what's happening in Hong Kong?" I told her what I had read.

"Oh, don't worry about this!" she exclaimed. "That's Hong Kong. It's not going to come here. The government has this under control."

Meanwhile, among the English, American, and Australian (Neil is English, Simon and I are American, and Maggie and Albert are Australian citizens originally from New Zealand) teachers at our college, we worried about what would happen during the first week of May. May 1 is Labor Day in China, and usually there is a weeklong holiday during which many, many people travel. College students all go home to visit their parents and friends in their hometowns, workers travel to visit their relatives, and many who can afford it visit "famous scenic spots" in China. Extra buses and trains (all of them jam-packed) are added to schedules, and people scramble to get all the available tickets. We knew that our two campuses have students from Beijing and Guangdong, so we worried about the students bringing back the SARS virus to our campus.

On Monday, April 21, I got a message from Neil and another one from Maggie on my telephone answering machine saying they had seen on the internet that the weeklong holiday had been cut to one day to discourage people from traveling. On Tuesday morning, I got a message from Effine that the holiday would be May 1 through May 5. I also received a message that the foreign teachers would attend a meeting about SARS to be held on Wednesday afternoon. The date was later changed to Thursday because of a conflict in Simon's schedule.

When I met with Mrs. Yu on Tuesday afternoon, I told her I had been very glad to hear that the holiday had been limited to one day, but then I was distressed to hear that now the holiday was five days long (including Saturday and Sunday).

"But the holiday must be at least three days legally, by l-a-w," she spelled. "And Saturday and Sunday happen to be the third and fourth of May.

"Mrs. Yu," I said, "if the students have five days, they are going to travel, and maybe they will go to Beijing or to Guangdong, and then they will bring the SARS virus back with them."

"No," she said, "because we will have a meeting with the students and tell them we hope they will not travel during this time." I didn't hold out much hope that the homesick students (most Chinese students are extremely sentimental about their parents and their hometowns) would pay any attention to the administration's "hopes."

New York Times, April 24:

The propaganda machine has been in high gear this week, with media coverage of SARS *newly* (emphasis mine) plentiful. But as usual during a crisis here, the points most emphasized by the propagandists are often a guide, in reverse, to the things the leaders most fear.

Today, as it became clear that Mr. Hu and fellow leaders faced public unease and a severe test of their ability to govern well, the front pages of the official *People's Daily* and other papers all carried a huge, hortatory article with the headline "In the Midst of Disaster, the Unity of the Masses Is an Impregnable Fortress."

A quote from Mr. Hu, from his courageous visit to Guangdong earlier this month, was highlighted: "A responsible government immediately places the interests of the people first."

On Thursday, April 24, I met Simon on the landing between our apartments. We met Neil, Maggie, and Albert in the lobby of the administration building and walked upstairs together. Mrs. Yu met us on the third floor and took us to a fancy conference room on the fourth floor. The foreign teachers sat at one end of the table. Mr. Yu (Mrs. Yu's boss, but no relation) sat at the head of the table at the opposite end. Mrs. Yu sat on his left and Effine to his right. Effine translated for Mr. Yu.

"We are faced with a serious situation with the SARS virus," Mr. Yu began, "and we would like to know what your thoughts and feelings about it are."

Silence. We looked at each other. "School first," Maggie said. "We would like to hear what the school has to say first."

Mr. Yu smiled condescendingly and opened a printed booklet. While he made his comments, Mr. Yu did not give us eye contact. He looked at his book, at the ceiling, at his hands. Mrs. Yu stared at the table or at him. Effine trembled nervously.

"Because Chinese officials did not realize the serious nature of this problem," he began, "this has aroused some international feelings." He then gave us some facts and figures, none of which were new to us. He next proceeded to tell us the symptoms of the disease and some recommendations for prevention. Then he began to tell us the measures that were being taken by the government to prevent the spread of the disease. And he admitted that a lack of information had led to some serious problems in Beijing.

"But," he said, "the officials were not covering up anything; they just didn't realize how serious it was."

I looked over at Maggie. Her smile froze; her eyes flashed.

After telling us about what the students were being required to do (they may not leave the campus overnight; in each dorm room of eight students, someone is appointed to monitor everyone's health and report any fever or coughing to their dean), Mr. Yu informed us that the city government had required all of the colleges and institutes to have this meeting with their foreign teachers. We were also told that the May holiday had now been limited to only one day. We would have classes as usual on every day except May 1. This one-day limit was apparently nationwide and applied to workers as well as students.

"If we want to leave, if we feel we are not comfortable staying here with this situation," Maggie began, "what is the school's position?"

"We know there were some mistakes in Beijing," Mr. Yu countered, "and we are learning from these mistakes. It's not going to get so bad here."

Albie tried again. "But what if we want to break our contract?"

Mr. Yu appeared flustered, and in the pause, I said quickly, my legal training coming to the fore, "I wouldn't say 'break,' if I were you, Albie."

"Really, it's not so serious," Mr. Yu pleaded. "In any case, we would have to see what the province recommends and what other schools are doing on this issue."

"So, who is going to make the decision?" Albie asked.

"It's not so serious," Mr. Yu repeated. "It's not as bad as Baghdad." He and Mrs. Yu snickered.

"What?" I said, almost jumping out of my chair. The five of us stared at them with confused shock on our faces.

"Nothing, nothing," Mr. Yu muttered.

"I would like to say that, in my opinion," Neil began, "we should have been having this meeting two months ago, and if the Chinese government had come forth with this information then instead of having nothing but the war on TV, then maybe we wouldn't have such a serious problem now."

"This is a problem," Mr. Yu nodded, and Mrs. Yu repeated, nodding, "Yes, this is a problem."

"At present there are only two cases in Jiangsu province," Effine said. Mr. Yu quickly and vehemently added something, and Effine translated, "And these are only suspected cases, not..." She paused, searching for the right word. "Confirmed," I prompted. Mr. Yu nodded vigorously.

My elbow jabbed Neil's arm. He had told me only the day before that a friend of his, a nurse in a Nanjing hospital, had said that someone had died of SARS in her hospital. He didn't choose to share that information at that moment.

"But there are people coming from Beijing and Guangdong every day," Neil pointed out. "They may be bringing the virus with them."

"Your concern is"—Mr. Yu paused—"reasonable."

"Well, I don't want to go," I said, feeling strong emotion. "All of us have to make our choices every day. What I want to know is, if I should have to be hospitalized, where will I be taken; no, not will, where would I be taken?"

Mr. Yu and Mrs. Yu looked at me for the first time during this meeting. "We don't want this! We don't think this will happen!" Mr. Yu almost shouted. Mrs. Yu's face softened.

"I hope it will not happen," I answered, "but will the school take responsibility for this if it comes to that?"

"Not only the school," Mr. Yu said, raising his arm and pointing to the ceiling, "but the government of China will take responsibility for this."

Mrs. Yu looked at me and smiled tenderly. "Don't worry about this…"

CHANGZHOU
2005

ANOTHER TRANSFORMATION

I am returning to Changzhou this time, not to teach but to visit friends and do some sightseeing.

I also am curious to see what changes have occurred in this ever-developing city. On my last visit, in 2002, the place had been transformed. Streets were widened with bicycle lanes; shade trees lined the walks; and park areas graced previously empty intersections. The drab six-story apartment buildings had been painted in lovely pastel colors; there were traffic lights at major intersections; and a Pizza Hut had been added to the Kentucky Fried Chicken and McDonald's.

Jiangsu Institute of Petrochemical Technology, my college, was also changing. A new women's dormitory was opened to accommodate the increased enrollment of women to the college. More important, in 2003, a new campus was planned and would become part of a College Park. JSIPT renamed itself Jiangsu Polytechnic Institute. The old campus would now serve graduate engineering and science students; the new campus would serve undergraduates. When I return this month, I shall visit the new campus with, so my friends there have told me, five new dorms and three new classroom buildings, all built between January 2003 and

October of that year and ready to house the freshmen and sophomore classes. I am eager to see the new classrooms; we foreign teachers suggested that several classrooms be set up as seminars with movable seats. The old classrooms had desks bolted to the floor, seats attached—not an ideal setup for conversational English. I have also been informed that Starbucks has come to Changzhou. I want to check out the prices and coffee types Starbucks is trying to sell Chinese customers. I suspect I shall use McD's and KFC for a cheap caffeine fix.

Most of all, I am looking forward to seeing friends. Two of my faculty students are now fathers; Yang Yan now heads the foreign affairs office and recruits teachers throughout Europe as well as arranging for student exchanges. Mr. Zhou now heads the English department, although he doesn't speak any English. Soon, there will be a lot to tell.

SOME SURPRISES

Going through customs in Shanghai, I was greeted by a sign informing me that if I had a cough, difficulty breathing, and a fever, I should immediately see a doctor, as there was a possibility of SARS. A second check had a similar warning but did not mention SARS. In Changzhou, however, there is no threat of the disease at this time.

My first surprise in my old home city here was the guest-house. Talk about dreaming of living in marble halls. The entrance sported big glass doors, a modern concierge desk, a row of clocks that displayed the times from various major cities around the world, and a tiled floor. The steps and all the halls were now tiled, and all the windows had been replaced. On the fifth floor, where most of the foreign teachers live, the dingy cement floors and the broken windows were gone. While I welcomed the change—somehow the six flights of stairs I must climb to get to my apartment don't seem as tiring as they did before—I'm not sure if it's the ambience that makes the steps seem lighter or if the reconstruction chopped off a few stairs on each flight. I have met most of the new teachers: Andre, from Canada; Peter, a Chinese American; Peter, from England; I'm told there is a Peter from Australia. It seems almost all the new teachers are named Peter; it must make everyone think that all foreign males are named Peter and somehow Andre's mother didn't favor him.

More streets have been widened since my last visit; more apartment buildings have been built; a new supermarket has come as well as a lovely park; and my old campus also has new buildings. The new campus, however, is something of a miracle. The southern part of Changzhou is now known as College Town or College Park. Jiangsu Polytechnic University, my home college, is one of six colleges in the new park. JPU's new campus will be home for undergraduate students, who now number more than eleven thousand—a big jump from the five thousand students here when I first came to the college. Students always said they were from a "small" college, but they can't say that now. College Park is still growing. By 2006, there will be a foreign affairs center, devoted to the foreign affairs office and to housing both foreign teachers and foreign students. Among the other colleges housed in the park are a communications university and a textile college. All of the colleges are architecturally distinct, and, as is happening all over China, trees abound, not only in campus parks but also along the streets.

Because the new college is a considerable distance from the old, most of the faculty have bought homes in the new area to avoid a more-than-forty-minute commute. There will be many more homes going up and, I hope, some restaurants. The teachers on the old campus prefer it there, as there are many places to eat and it is a short bus ride to the center of town.

I have not yet checked out Starbucks, but Peter from England, whom I know from my previous stay here, tells me it is pricey. At the same time, I learned from television that coffee is becoming popular among the young—part of being like the West. I am happy, though, that my little market still functions, and I have walked through it twice already.

NEW CHALLENGE AT THE INTERNET CAFÉ

China Notes is about to become *China Fragments*. The internet keeps cutting off my columns, and yesterday, for the fourth time, I lost everything I had written. It takes me a good hour to regain my calm.

I am here in China this time to visit many friends as well as to visit Guilin. Seeing friends also means eating many delicious meals. I am not only reacquainting myself with favorite foods but am also trying some new ones (the shift key sticks here, so, readers, you may have to supply a few capitals yourselves). Among the old-time delicacies are duck's tongue and silver fish; the former was prepared with one of the best sauces I have ever tasted with the tongue—a really palatable part of the duck—and the silver fish was served both in soups and in egg dishes. It is a very small white fish with not a fish taste and in eggs adds an extra bit of protein.

The new treats included a fried fish, about the size of a guppy, very crispy, and one eats it whole. I have also had quail stomachs served with greens that are in season now. I shall probably experience a few more new dishes when I go south to Guilin, as foods vary somewhat with the region. I've read in the guidebooks that snake is a favorite dish in this area of China, but I shall avoid it.

As a gift of sorts, I was taken to see Taihu, a lovely lake in Wuxi, a city that borders part of Changzhou. Its waters serve as a freshwater source for part of China. I don't know, however, how long this lake will remain unpolluted. As the area is scenic, more hotels and expensive housing are being built along the lakeshore; additionally, a golf course has been built along the lake's edge. I think how much the Sherman Inland-Wetlands Commission devoted to keeping the planned golf course in Sherman free from fertilizers and pesticides to prevent polluting the Housatonic river and know this will not be the case in China. I spotted both garbage and phragmites along the lake banks, meaning the water is not well-protected either from humans or invasive plants.

Thursday, I leave for Guilin. I am traveling with a Chinese group; to do so meant signing a statement that I was willing to travel with a Chinese group. I asked why the Chinese didn't have to sign a statement saying they were willing to travel with me.

Next week, James Soong, of Taiwan's People's First Party, will do a repeat of the trip of KMT leader Lien Chan. I hope when I return to Sherman, I can persuade the JCC to let me talk about the political implications of what is happening here. These visits are part of power politics, and the United States is one of the players, though not visibly.

GETTING REACQUAINTED

My first morning in Changzhou, I woke to the sounds of a band and knew a funeral procession was taking place. Sure enough, on the street below, there was a group of mourners; the women in white head-dresses—white a color of mourning here—led the procession. They were followed by a coffin draped in red. The red signified that the deceased had led a long and happy life. If a young person or child dies, the coffin is draped in white. Last in line was the band, mostly tubas and other brass instruments. Once the funeral rites have taken place, the family will host a feast. In small villages, the whole village is invited, but here in the city, the family will serve their apartment complex. The daughters-in-law are supposed to wail and tear their hair, which must be difficult if the old mother-in-law was a bit of a dragon.

Yesterday, I went to the Buddhist temple here, one of my favorite places in the city. The temple is the oldest in the province, one of four old temples in China, according to Mr. Gao, one of my former faculty students. The garden areas at the temple are lovely and provide a quiet, peaceful place to read or just sit. When I am fortunate enough to hit the times right, I am treated to chanting. Luck was with me, and there was quite a ceremony going on. From what I gathered, this was a special prayer group. The monks were dressed in red and wore elaborate crowns; bells and drumbeats accompanied their chanting. A group of people also sat in the room, making me think the prayers were for this particular family.

I have been told that there were several other Buddhist temples in the city, but most were destroyed during the Cultural Revolution, along with churches. How this survived is something of a miracle. The monastery does well financially. Along with an entrance price of fifteen yuan (about two dollars), they sell incense and souvenirs. The main "chapel" houses a giant Buddha, who is surrounded by the four heavenly kings. The kings are part of Chinese folklore. Supposedly the Yellow Emperor, China's mythical founder, delegated some responsibility to the four kings. They guard the four comers of the universe; each has special qualities and is associated with a different color. Although I have called the Yellow Emperor a mythical figure, his reality is actually ambiguous. Historians don't seem certain about his existence.

The Labor Day holiday begins May 1 and will last a week. I shall stay put during this time as the rest of China is on the move. Booking tickets for trains, buses, and hotels is almost impossible. I shall head for Guilin the following week. Here in Changzhou, the weather is steamy and will be even hotter in Guilin. This area, however, is particularly beautiful and is said to inspire the dreamy Chinese paintings of mountains hung with mist and surrounded by water.

For those of you new to my title of Venerable Foreign Expert, this note. Foreign teachers are known as foreign experts here, and since on my first visit to China I was the oldest teacher, I was treated with great respect, thus, Venerable Foreign Expert.

SOME INFORMATION ABOUT BUDDHISM

Buddhism began in India, but it found its home in China. Another immigrant from India was the Monkey King, whose origin is the monkey god Hanuman, found in the great Hindu epic the Ramayana. Hanuman had two great powers: enormous strength and the ability to go anywhere in the world in an instant. However, he did not have much of a brain; sent to the mountains to bring back a magical plant, he was unable to remember the plant, so he brought home the whole mountain. Unlike Hanuman, the Monkey King of China was very clever. He was also very naughty, like so many of the trickster gods that populate world myths. His story can be found in *Journey to the West*. The monkey is also part of the Chinese zodiac, and those born in the year of the monkey are said to be very clever but somewhat tricky and untrustworthy.

But back to the Buddha. If you visit a Buddhist temple or monastery, you will see the Buddha surrounded by four towering figures, each with a different-colored face. I had no idea what they were or what they represented until Yang Yan's husband, Mr. Ji, told me they are the four kings who guard the four corners of the earth. They are part of Chinese folklore incorporated into Buddhism. Zhuan Xu, the black-faced king, guards the north, while Yang Dai of the red face guards the south. He is in charge of the summer, just as Zhuan Xu is in charge of the winter. To the east and overseer of spring stands Tai Hao of the green face; his counterpart is Shao Hao, guardian of the west with his white face, who oversees autumn. These four kings also appear in Daoist temples. As for the color yellow, it belongs to Huangdi, the Yellow Emperor, who is said to be the founder of China. He has four faces, so nothing can escape his gaze. The color yellow belongs to the emperors of China

Here, from the "Song of Eternal Sorrows," by Bai Juyi:

> In Heaven we shall be birds
> Flying side by side
> On earth flowering sprigs
> On the same branch.

A lovely poem to send for a Valentine.

I MEET AUSTRALIAN PETER

I am living in one of the two apartments on the sixth floor of the guesthouse. The apartments are lovely, having an additional room to join the bedroom, bath, and a small kitchen complete with refrigerator and microwave. As far as I knew, I was the lone resident on the floor. Then, one day as I was opening my door, a trim man came bounding up the stairs two at a time. I was astonished. I have mentioned that the stairs between floors are each two flights, and we foreign teachers used to joke about a need for a way station similar to those set up by climbers to Mt. Everest. This man turned out to be Peter Hayes, a sixty-something Australian in good shape.

Peter introduced himself and said he had been hoping to meet me and say hello and apologized that it had taken so long. He asked me to join him for dinner that evening. I learned he was ex-military and after retiring had taken an MBA degree. He was now in Changzhou doing consulting work. He proved to be an interesting and intelligent dinner companion, and we shared several dinners in the new restaurant that had been set up next to the guesthouse.

Something I found ingenious was Peter's solution to ordering his dinners. He had purchased a Chinese cookbook with photographs of dishes and lists of ingredients. He would show this to the waiter and indicate he wanted something like this. I introduced him to some of the foods whose names I had learned. We always went Dutch treat.

One thing we both agreed was that news on the Chinese TV was superior to the news accounts we had in our home countries. The top story, of course, was about Jiang Zemin, the president, but then became worldwide with stories about Africa, South America, Europe, and the United States. Watching the news in China treated the viewer to the goings-on of the world. Chinese TV newscasts reminded me of the magazine *World Press*, which I once subscribed to. It provided me with points of view from other countries in the world and was an eye-opener.

I always enjoyed the dinners and conversations I had with Peter.

RELEARNING THINGS

Because so many streets have been widened in Changzhou, I am having to relearn landmarks. Yesterday, I missed the stop for the Times supermarket and had to walk back from the next stop. Along with the wider streets have come more traffic lights, and signals there now display little green men to signal go and little red ones to say stay put. This has not made crossing the streets any safer, however. Turning traffic and cars that disregard the stoplights make going from one side of the street to the next a hazardous undertaking. I have reverted to my old system, crossing mid-street or placing myself in the middle of a group of people and crossing with them.

Last night, I gave a talk to the English majors, and anyone else who wished, on American college students. I believe it went well, as I was kept far beyond the scheduled time. Students, usually so reticent about speaking, asked many questions. Several came up after class to request visiting with me. I always say yes. I not only think it is part of what I should give here but also enjoy talking with students. I learn a lot about young people here. It is a bit like meeting myself when I was a college student.

Tonight, I am dining with Mr. Gao, one of the faculty I taught my first year here. He introduced himself to me and his classmates with "I am an ugly man. Even my wife says I am an ugly man." It's true but also true is that he's lovable. Mr. Gao is a country boy from a poor family. To go to middle school, he had to walk several hours from his home to school. This meant staying at the school from Sunday evening to Friday afternoon, when he would walk back home. My reason for enjoying Mr. Gao, however, is that he is both an excellent student and a lot of fun. He came into my English class in the second semester and, within the week, was giving out answers to his classmates. Once, I handed out slips of questions—what-ifs—for the students to talk about to their classmates. Mr. Yu's question was "what if you had a million dollars?" He became flustered; it was too much money for him to deal with. "Maybe," I said, "your classmates can help you spend some." His classmates traveled with his extra money, bought things, gave to charity. When it came to Mr. Gao, he said, "I will buy him some concubines."

Poor Mr. Yu went red while the rest of the class laughed.

I also bumped into Mr. Wu's mother-in-law, who took me by the hand to the Wu home. Mr. Wu was another of my faculty English class. He often invited me to his home for dinner, and I learned many new foods to buy at the markets. At dinner, Mr. Wu and his wife made up a list of the foods we were eating along with the characters, their meanings, and the pinyin (or English terms). My memory, not great with the years, served me well these times, however. Mr. Wu was also a poor boy from a farm; he was also very intelligent and went to Beijing University, as difficult to enter as Harvard or Princeton. He was also there during the Tiananmen protests. He said he did not take part, but I feel this must have been a very unnerving time for him.

From television, I have learned that Changzhou has China's first horticultural center. Flowers and trees

have become a big business here, and the center provides information on species, care, and planting. At a
flower center in Xiaxi, experiments with tree varieties
are ongoing. Trees that grow quickly and well in the
poor soils of the country's Yellow River area are particularly important. The desert has been encroaching
there, and the pollution in Beijing is often the product
of desert sand storms. Other than this, the big news
here is the visit of the Kuomintang party leader, the
first since the end of the Civil War in 1949.

VISITORS FROM TAIWAN

For eight days now, I have been following the visit to
China of Lien Chan, head of the Kuomintang Party in
Taiwan. His visit marks the first time Chan has been
to the mainland since 1949 and the first time that the
KMT and the Communist Party have met since the
end of the Civil War. Chan's visit began in Nanjing,
the home of the KMT and its founder, Sun Yatsen.
Both the KMT and the Communists pay respect to
Sun Yatsen, who established the first democratic state
here. There is an impressive museum and tomb to him
in Nanjing, and it was a fine place for Chan to begin
his journey. The next stop was Beijing, where Chan
met with Hu Jintao, head of the Communist Party. The
"noises" from this meeting were promising—a declara-
tion that the past was the past, and it was now time to
build a future together. Chan's party, however, is not

in power nor is the People's First Party, whose head will soon make a visit here. The leader of the party in power in Taiwan is for an independent Taiwan, and the thinking here is that with two parties favoring a move to a united China, the third party will have to yield. It will be interesting to see how this develops.

There are about a million Taiwanese working in Shanghai, and Taiwan is a main investor in mainland businesses. This week, the first direct flights began from the mainland to Taiwan. Although a move to reunification is promising, it will take time. The Communist Party will most likely offer the same accommodations to Taiwan as it has to Hong Kong and Macao.

I don't know how much is reported at home about the many accords going on between China and India and between Japan and India as well as between Japan and Pakistan. There is real political gamesmanship going on here, with the United States as a silent partner with Japan. The Chinese are uneasy about Japan, and the United States is uneasy with Communist China. The situation bears watching, but I doubt it will be a story at home.

China Central Television (CCTV) is an all-English channel, and Peter the Australian and I feel it offers far superior coverage of the world than anything either of us sees at home. We not only receive news from all of Asia but receive news of Europe, Africa, and the

United States. True, there is often a slant. A recent celebration in Vietnam, marking the end of the war with the United States, is presented as a celebration of Vietnam's victory over us. This isn't exactly how the story would be presented by our media. Along with a broader range of news stories, CCTV offers cultural programs, history, and travelogues. I learn a lot about China from this channel.

I have been seeing many old friends here, the majority the faculty to whom I taught English. Last evening, I had lunch with Mr. Peng and Mr. Liu and their families. Both Peng and Liu were friends and single when I taught them. Mr. Liu met his wife midway through the course. Because marriage age for college faculty is twenty-five for the man and twenty-three for the woman, he had to wait a few years for her to meet the age requirement. It was Mr. Liu's wedding that I attended the last time I was here. Both men have had sons, a good thing. Their friendship has some friendly competition, and Mr. Liu would have been in for some teasing if he had had a girl.

Food, as always, was great. Had some duck's tongue again and wonderful fish cakes. Best of all was seeing my former students so happy with their families.

MORE OF THE TAIWAN VISITS

Here we are on the sticky-letter computer again, not by choice but by necessity. these last weeks have been emotional ones here, beginning with the visits of the Taiwanese party leaders, chan and soong. fifty-six years have elapsed since the two have been to the mainland, and their itineraries included stops at their ancestral homes, where they paid respect to their grandparents and parents. they were welcomed by the schools they had attended as children, and chan had a difficult time controlling his tears, and even after his trip, when interviewed, he choked up when he talked about Xi'an, his boyhood home.

Their visits were followed by a memorial to the Holocaust. the television program acknowledged the horror of that time, but there was also a dig at the Japanese, along with footage from the atrocities of the Japanese troops; the program then focused on germany's apology and its acknowledgement of its wrongdoing. the voice-over said germany had come to grips with its history; the unstated message was that Japan had not, a very sore point with both the Chinese and Koreans.

This week, the sixtieth anniversary of the end of WWII, Japanese war crimes took a top spot in Chinese television coverage of the ceremonies. I thought the rape of Nanjing, where more than three hundred thousand civilians were massacred, would lead, but that wasn't the case. Instead, the story concentrated on other areas; one survivor in a small village recalled the mass killings of women and children. In another place, which the Chinese hope will become a world heritage spot, a museum has been built in the building where the japanese conducted biological experiments on the Chinese. This part of the japanese occupation of china gets little press, but the medical experiments here were as horrifying as those done in the Nazi camps. Little wonder that it still rankles that the Japanese not only refuse to offer an apology but have obliterated japanese responsibility for the war in their latest textbooks. The demonstrations in beijing and shanghai reported here and at home bear witness to the anger that remains here.

Other than this, I have been sharing dinners with australian peter and last night met one of the other australian teachers here in changzhou. an interesting man. John has been teaching here on and off since 1993, so we had a good time comparing teaching notes with each other; the food was not the greatest and was definitely overpriced, but the company was stimulating,

THE HOLIDAY CRUSH

Today is Sunday, and administrators are back in the office today, and students are making up classes. Here, if time is given for a holiday, some of the time must be made up, and often makeup time involves a weekend. There are three main holidays that offer time—Spring Festival, National Day, and Labor Day—and they are known as golden periods because they allow families to get together or to travel. This year, the golden periods seemed less than golden. The reason I did not go to Guilin during the Labor Day holiday is because of the crowding and high prices. Tickets on planes, buses, and trains charge higher prices, and so do hotels and restaurants. There are long lines for all museums, historic places, and parks. Chinese interviewed on television felt they were better off staying home.

I spent the holiday time with old friends. My day with the Wu family included an introduction to Qigong. This form of exercise is quite interesting; it involves small movements of the body but provides a real workout. Mr. Wu made a DVD copy of the exercises for me, and I intend to keep at it once I get home. Qi is the individual's vital force, and in one of the small exercises, I could actually feel this force. An interesting experience for usually skeptical me. I think, once I have practiced, I shall feel this force in other parts of my body. Along with trying Qigong, I ate my first quail eggs. These are very delicious, and I hope do not have as high cholesterol as ordinary eggs, as the Wus kept piling them on my plate.

I also spent time with the Gu family. I shall have to identify everyone by his or her relationship in the family. In China, I am seldom given names. "This is my aunt." "This is my father's brother." My favorite name, however, is "bamboo uncle," known this way as he paints bamboo. I spent the early part of the day with the Gu grandparents and offspring. Grandfather Gu once again took me into the courtyard to practice calligraphy on the walls, using water for ink. They recognized my characters, and once we practiced on the wall, we went inside to work on paper. I have several examples of calligraphy, all larger than the characters I have been working on at home. The family thought my small characters were quite good. Grandfather Gu and Bamboo Uncle said they could not work in small characters. I have a difficult time with the large ones.

After a wonderful lunch, we were off to Taihu in nearby Wuxi. The lake is surrounded by hills, all forested, and the area is known for its beauty. Sited against the hills stands an eighty-eight-meter statue of the Buddha. He is a standing figure as opposed to the usually seated Buddhas of the temples here, and the placement of his hands signifies peace. We had dinner on one of the boats docked at the lake and, as one would expect, had lots of fish dishes.

Well, before this disappears, I'm off to the administration building to check on my trip to Guilin.

GUILIN AT LAST

The traveler to Guilin has a lot to forgive. The city itself is unattractive, and the tours include more commercial than scenic attractions. Between every visit to a cave or park, the guide stopped the group at a store where everything from tea, jade, diamonds, Chinese medicine, and fish was sold. What made this all worthwhile, however, was the boat trip down the Lijiang (Li River). Here stand the misty mountains, which erosion has shaped into incredible forms. Like snowflakes and fingerprints, no two mountains are the same. Along the river as the boat moves away from the city of Guilin, a traveler can see paths from the villages to the river and women washing clothes or fetching water. Rafts, so often pictured in Chinese paintings, line the banks. This was what I came to Guilin to see, and I would love to kayak or canoe down the Lijiang to become one with the scenery.

One of the mountains has eroded into a shape of a camel. It is known both as Camel Hill and as Clinton Camel Hill because the former president gave a speech here on the environment. Another hill resembles an elephant drinking water from the river and, as with many Chinese sites, has a story attached to it. According to legend, the Jade Emperor abandoned a sick elephant on the banks of the Li River. The local people nursed it back to health, and as the elephant loved the mountain and river, it stayed on earth. When the emperor discovered this, he sent his heavenly troops to catch the elephant, but the elephant didn't submit. Then, a soldier thrust a dagger into the elephant's back. The elephant didn't fall but turned to a stone hill to guard the people of Guilin forever. One can still see the dagger in the elephant's back—actually, the pagoda that has been built there. The elephant is the symbol of Guilin.

Two of the many shops the tour visited were of interest to me. One was the fish place, where there was every kind of fish in all various forms: dried, slivered, powdered, formed into many cubes of different tastes. Each kind of fish was offered in small bowls for the customer to taste. Some had interesting tastes, and some I avoided.

The second shop offered all forms of Chinese medicine: leaves, mushrooms, dried animals of every kind. One tray held samples of what I took to be sesame seeds but on closer inspection turned out to be black ants. The ants were also available in boxes. I saw many large vats, generally full of black liquid; customers could sample the contents. I tried the mushroom tea, which I found quite refreshing. I followed this with black-ant wine. Black-ant wine has a terrific punch, like a high-proof cognac, and reminded me of the Barney Google comic's kickapoo joy juice. I'm not sure what the wine was good for, but I'm certain I would have been told it was good for my health. Several other vats with black liquid revealed snakes and other creatures; these, too, would be good for my health, but I preferred to gamble with my fate and passed tasting these.

At this place, the group was ushered into a room for a sales pitch before being allowed to shop the area. The salespeople reminded me of some of the late-show sales pitches shown on early television, and perhaps some of you may remember the man who pitched a knife that sliced with ease through tomatoes, carrots, and eventually a piece of metal, all showing that the knife retained its edge. Although I didn't understand a word at the various shops, I enjoyed the show. I also sampled some unknown items, and I think that lack of information was for the best.

SOME FACTS ABOUT HAIR

Of course there are bald men in China, but they are a minority, and most American men would do cartwheels to have the thick black mops of Chinese men. Not many men have gray hair here either, but that's because the majority dye their hair. Women, on the other hand, don't always dye their hair, and I have seen some beautiful white heads on Chinese grandmothers. Vanity in China belongs to the male.

Among the young, changing hair color and style is more prevalent. Girls generally keep their locks long and straight, perhaps because TV commercials for shampoo show long, straight, gleaming black tresses. Long enough, by the way, to produce Chinese Lady Godivas. Few young people perm their hair, but older women opt for some curl; so do a few boys. The more adventurous young people also dye their hair, and to my mind, the orange color—sometimes streaks and sometimes whole head—isn't pretty. I saw one young man who had managed not only to curl his hair but also to reduce the color to a light blond. Not too bad.

Since my last visit here, the number of cars has proliferated. At the apartment complex where Yang Yan lives, I saw few cars parked there in my 2002–2003 teaching stint. This time cars lined the streets, filled any empty space available, and also filled garages. These last cost a lot of money, so the increase in cars is evidence of the growing economy in Changzhou. The city is one of the industrial enterprise areas south of the Yangzi, and its sister cities of Wuxi and Suzhou are also growing. As for Shanghai, new apartments are being built everywhere, and people continue to move into the city along with an increasing number of cars. The cars are not cheap—BMW, Audi, Mercedes-Benz are common, although VW is most prevalent. If anyone wishes to know what overpopulation is like, a visit to Shanghai can provide all the information one needs.

It is difficult to walk on the streets or get onto the metro and buses, and the pushing and shoving don't do much for one's temperament. Despite all the people and cars, however, it is easy to cross the streets—this is because traffic jams make possible the chance to cross the road at almost any point on a street. Lights really aren't necessary for the Shanghai pedestrian. Here in Changzhou, however, the street lights are of little help; right and left turns make the journey from one side of the street to the other something like the challenge of a bull fight.

Among other changes here and in Shanghai is the popularity of coffee. Several coffee shops in addition to Starbucks have opened, and in the supermarkets, coffee products line the shelves, everything from instant and decaf to lattes and cappuccinos. Someday, the United States may not only be vying with China for oil but also for coffee. I am, by the way, seeing more fat children here—fast foods and snacks, which people find tasty, are doing to Chinese children what they are doing to American children.

FAREWELL ONCE MORE

I'm homeward bound once again. I've met with my former faculty friends for a goodbye feast. It has been a pleasure to see how well they are all doing and how their careers are progressing. I haven't talked about the college president, Mr. Chen, but I found him to be one of the best administrators I have ever worked with. First, there was Yang Yan. All of us foreign experts recognized she was the real head of the Foreign Affairs office. She was made head of the department. Guan Chunying, previously a librarian, was appointed head of personnel; Mr. Peng became a college administrator, and Mr. Gao also became a department head. These were some of the brightest and most capable of my faculty students, and I admired President Chen for seeing their abilities. I had occasion to talk to him once at lunch, and I found that one of the things he introduced on the new campus was a faculty dining room. Mr. Zhou was put in charge of this, not only because he was capable but also to salve his feelings about being transferred out of the Foreign Affairs office. President Chen initiated the faculty dining room to help faculty meet members of other departments, although he noted each department seemed to stick to its own people. He also commented that people still complained, and I said that at home even when we had a good administrator, we found something to complain about. Human nature doesn't respect national borders.

As always, I leave for home with mixed feelings. I only wish the trip to and from China was as short as the trips to England or France. I would take it more often.

CHANGZHOU
2008

A LAST TEACHING TRIP

Once again, I'm off to China. The city and school are the same, but with major differences. Changzhou, which I first came to in 2000, was a city of bicycles, dowdy buildings, rickety buses, and few foreigners. The university, then known as Jiangsu School of Petrochemical Technology, had only five thousand students. Located in a far comer of the city, the college was surrounded by small shops, restaurants, and two markets.

My last visit to China in 2005 witnessed one of those development wonders that visitors marvel at. Changzhou is now a city of wide tree-lined avenues, new as well as spruced-up buildings, modern air-conditioned buses, and cars, cars, cars.

The school, too, has changed. It is now known as Jiangsu Polytechnic University, and the old campus has become a graduate research facility. A new campus, built for undergraduates, has become part of College Park, where six universities have been built, each with its own distinct architecture. JPU's students now number nearly thirteen thousand.

I shall be teaching five classes of oral English: three classes for computer science students and two for environmental science students. Fortunately, in my years as an editor, I worked on a number of computer texts, and workshops for inland-wetland commissioners schooled me in many ecological concerns. I won't be completely working in unfamiliar territory. Learning the new campus and the new bus routes into town will be a challenge, however. I am not sure, either, how popular American teachers will be now or if students are as respectful of their professors as they once were.

I do know that I shall see many old friends, eat many wonderful meals, and meet many new adventures. I look forward to all of these and, if time permits, shall take Chinese lessons, one of the new perks offered to foreign experts.

THIS YEAR'S FOREIGN TEACHERS

There are eleven foreign teachers here, nine of them men and two of us women. The other woman is from Japan, here teaching Japanese and not speaking any English. We live in the campus guesthouse, and living accommodations are excellent. Nothing has been spared to make us comfortable. On the fifth floor where we live, there are two kitchens, both outfitted with pots, pans, woks, dishes, and silverware as well as tables and chairs. The laundry room sports two washing machines and plenty of drying lines. This as opposed to the one washing machine on the old campus and drying lines that constantly fell down with the weight of the clothes. In addition, there is now heating in the laundry room, making clean clothes a short wait. The college has given us an extra sheet just in case our used one doesn't dry on time. The towels are thick and absorbent, unlike those I had in my early days in China.

The school has given us many perks. For instance, we can now buy bus cards, giving us a fare reduction. We have been given cards for the dining halls, which provide up to four yuan toward our lunch or dinner. And we have ATM cards; when our salaries are deposited, we can retrieve our money at a college ATM machine. In a short time, we shall be given a welcoming banquet; those are marvelous, and all the high officers of the college, including the president, will be there to welcome us.

For me, one benefit I enjoy is the elevator; many buildings now have them. Classrooms, however, are still unheated. I have a good-sized room, outfitted with a bed, desk, wardrobe, and several end tables and chairs; I also have my own bathroom. Each room has a bay window with floor-to-ceiling windows; that's where I sit mornings to have my tea and watch the boys practice basketball, a big sport here. In addition to about twenty basketball courts, there are approximately four badminton courts, badminton being another popular sport here.

The university now has fifteen thousand students on this campus and one thousand teachers. The old campus is a graduate science facility. This year, Jiangsu Polytechnic University will celebrate its thirtieth anniversary and plans a big ceremony. I'm glad to be here for this.

Since my last visit, apartments and little restaurants have sprouted up. I was told that the outlying areas of Changzhou have become entire mini cities and what was once downtown is no longer a center hub. One addition to the city is a Walmart. The store joins McDonald's, Kentucky Fried Chicken, Pizza Hut, and Starbucks.

OLD FRIENDS, NEW ADVENTURES

I have met with a dear friend here. Xu Ping is one of the Chinese English teachers, and we spent Wednesday chatting and seeing her new home. A new housing complex has been built a short bus ride from the campus, a good part of it designed for the university faculty. Many have chosen to move rather than spend a forty-minute ride from the old university to this new one. Faculty houses are the traditional six-story buildings; Xu Ping has a duplex on the fifth floor, so the climb was not as bad as I expected.

Xu Ping's mother is living there and prepared the lunch, my first real Chinese meal and most welcome. Afterward, Xu Ping's mother began to fold ghost money. April 7 is Tomb Sweeping Day, a holiday that honors one's ancestors, and paper money is burned at the graves of the departed ancestors. This money eases their lives in the next world.

Folding the money into what results as boat-shaped currency takes a bit of doing, and I was not too successful at it. Two red and yellow squares make the big money; silver and gold sheets make up the smaller money. All this work will be burned on Tomb Sweeping Day.

At the old campus in the bai yun district, I often joined Xu Ping in the evening to dance at the square beside her home. This is good exercise, so I was happy to learn that women also dance in an area in the new complex. This Friday, I'll join both Xu Ping and her mother for dancing. This is a woman's exercise; men don't join because, Xu Ping laughed, "They are a little lazy."

Since my visit here in 2005, both apartment houses and small stores have filled in the empty fields. I join the students in having my meals at the stores across the street from the campus—a hazardous undertaking as there is no traffic light, and pedestrians don't rule here. There are several traditional noodle and dinner places, but learning how to negotiate the newer places has taken some getting used to. At the soup dumpling place, the price is set by the number of dumplings in the soup. My last bowl cost three yuan—a bit less than fifty cents and I was stuffed. At other places, the customer takes a plastic bowl, fills it with vegetables and meatballs, and hands it to the "cook." He or she places it in a boiling stock, which, when done, is one's meal. A favorite of mine and many of the students is a vegetable wrap. Again, one picks out an assortment of chopped vegetables, which are stir-fried, sometimes with an egg or meat, and placed on a pita-sized wrap. These are good and filling as well, costing the equivalent of forty cents. All the vendors and cooks know me as I am always saying, "Bu yan, bu weijing, bu tang," or "no salt, no MSG, and no sugar."

Shopping for foodstuffs and other household items means a bus ride to TESCO, a supermarket. This is not as good as the Times, where I shopped in the bai yun district. Walmart offers better foods and a wider variety of household goods.

My classes begin on Monday, March 3, and that evening the foreign teachers will have their welcoming banquet.

THE MONKEY KING CLUB

This has been a week or excursions. Andre, a basket-ball-player-tall Canadian who has been teaching here for three years, took two of us to the Monkey King. This night spot is named after the trickster character in the Chinese classic *Journey to the West*. The "club" caters to foreigners and apparently has an international reputation as one of the places to visit. I had never heard of it, however, in any of my earlier visits to China. The food is Western, including a decent-looking pizza, and like all Western food costs more than it should. My tea alone cost me five yuan, enough actually to buy me two meals here on campus. The restaurant was opened by a Palestinian, and the clientele is United Nations rich. Andre knows everyone, and it seems everyone knows Andre. On Friday nights, there are poker games, and according to Andre, some of the players are local big shots, who play for big money. On Saturday nights, there are mahjongg games—these also played for money. Players put up fifteen yuan to play and during the game are given tea and snacks. If I were a young teacher here, I would go not to gamble but to meet so many people from all over the world.

The next excursion took us to the tallest building in Changzhou. This was a celebration of Women's Day and included not only the women but administrators, party members and faculty. At the top of the building is a restaurant that features an all-you-can-eat buffet for one hundred yuan (about fifteen dollars) and whose floor revolves. A customer can view the entire city of Changzhou, which takes about an hour to make a complete cycle. Unfortunately, Women's Day turned out to be rainy and foggy, so the viewing was not spectacular. After stuffing ourselves and toasting everyone, the foreign teachers were taken to the City Planning Bureau of Changzhou. The city has one of the most ancient settlements in China, and there were both photographs and models of the city. These ranged from ancient times to proposals for the future. Most interesting to me, because of sitting on the Inland-Wetlands Commission, were the proposals for treating waste and purifying the water. These included waste management buildings and water purification centers. Both waste and water are big problems here. The subway system will be expanded, and the city will convert from coal to natural gas.

One system for water purification was modeled after a program in South America and one in Upstate New York, where a planting of reeds and rushes was used to purify runoff water.

Between outings, I met my first classes. The students of one have all taken English names; another clapped for me. I tell them I am the oldest teacher in China and, like their grandparents, am patient and kind, both needed to get students to feel comfortable speaking English.

A NEWS ARTICLE ON IRAN

China Daily, the international English-language paper, recently published a four-page supplement on Iran, celebrating the twenty-ninth national day of the Islamic Republic of Iran. The top story on page one of the supplement celebrated the steady growth of Sino-Iranian ties. The article noted that both Iran and China had long histories and were both cradles of civilization. China's history dates back nearly six thousand years and Iran's more than two thousand years to the Persian empire. The Silk Road connected the two countries for twenty centuries.

Americans should find the following quote from the article most interesting: "The government of Iran, like the leaders of China, reiterates the importance of justice, clemency and friendship in international relationships, and believe that equal status of states in the world community does not allow any country to exploit, intimidate or dictate policies to other states on the basis of unilateral practices improvised by any such state."

This is China's polite way of criticizing what is known as American hegemony. The statement is similar to that of Jiang Zemin on his travels throughout South America in 2000. While the United States was bogged down in the election controversy and then the Iraq war, the Chinese were cementing relationships in Latin America and Africa. And, although saddled with some economic problems of its own, China broadcast the idea that Third World countries should help other Third World countries. Partly, this is propaganda, and effective propaganda, but China's one objective is trade, whereas ours depends on who supports America or what regimes aid us in controlling other parts of the world we see as vital to our interests. Readers can decide which policy may prove better in the long run.

Other articles, most written with the aid of the Iranian embassy in China, noted that Iran ranks second in production among oil and gas nations and has 16.13 per cent of the world's reserves.

Iran's chief trading partners were China, Japan, Germany, Italy, and the Republic of Korea. The paper also ran an August 2007 photo of Hu Jintao and Ahmadinejad shaking hands. And just in case you wondered about women's role in Iran, another article said Iranian women were finding their place in the sun.

Since my last writing, I have been taking my meals at the faculty cafeteria. The offerings are not great, but I take a big lunch and go across the road to the little restaurants for a dinner of soup or dumplings. I have met with many of the faculty I once worked with or taught, and my former faculty students and I have planned a get-together for dinner. My new students are a good group and as usual have offered up such English names as Stone, Sun, and Cloud.

STUDENTS AND COLLEGE

I have told my classes, all of them sophomores in various computer and science courses, that I am the oldest teacher in China—unless you count Confucius, long dead. Here, unless they have reached the rank of full professor, women teachers must retire at fifty-five years of age and men at sixty. Those who have become full professors may add five years to their retirement age. By Chinese rules, I am far beyond teaching age

Tuition and fees at the university also vary. For students who have passed the entrance exams at good or better scores, tuition is four thousand yuan, about $550, for the year. For students who have passed below the acceptable score, but not below a set amount, tuition is six thousand yuan. It does not pay to be a dumb or a lazy student. Add to these amounts twelve hundred yuan for room and whatever the parents can send for food. There are several campus dining halls (canteens) for students, and they may buy cards to pay for their meals; meals vary in both quality and price. Most students elect to go across the street to the little restaurants and food vendors that line an alley off the street. The food is cheaper and more interesting.

Since the university has established a program for students going abroad to Western universities—as well as programs for foreigners wishing to study in China— there is still another price for tuition: twenty-one thousand yuan (about three thousand dollars). This is a hefty bite for Chinese families and does not account for the cost of going to a foreign university. The program is housed in its own building, and one of the privileges of teaching or studying there is heated classrooms in winter and air-conditioning in spring and summer.

A week ago, some of the faculty I taught my first year in China gathered to say hello and treat me to dinner. They have decided to do this once a month—they say to practice English, but they go on in Chinese. Dinner was in the bai yun district, where I first taught, and before dinner we walked around the old campus, now another school. I went to one of my favorite places, the campus's little garden. The walk to the garden is lined with plum trees, all in blossom. On nice mornings or after lunch, I often sat there. Generally, there were students walking around with books in their hands and reciting their lessons. They always reminded me of *Fahrenheit 451*. Other times, I met students in the garden for conversation. I do miss that place.

The college had two gardens; this one, the little garden was my favorite place to meet students and to relax.

I am having Chinese lessons. I have been told that I have a young heart in an old body; I have to see where the brain fits in.

CONSTANT CONSTRUCTION

I haven't mentioned the dust here, fine sandlike granules that seep through the windows and our heating units. A day's accumulation would permit me to do my calligraphy on the furniture tops; two days' accumulation on the floors produces dust bunnies. Dusting and sweeping become daily chores.

The source of so much dust I have attributed to the constant construction in this area; outside my window, I can see at least three new buildings going up. On the roads into the center of town, the new buildings being erected are too numerous to count. This district, known as the Wujin area of Changzhou, is the fastest-growing part of the city.

Wujin is also known as the home of College Park; six universities have campuses here. Building began in 2003. By 2005, six colleges had been constructed. Little else existed except vacant fields. No longer. Today, the empty fields house apartments and homes for the faculty and other workers in the area. Each campus has its garden and body of water: a pond, a stream, a lake. Walking with Seki, the Japanese teacher here, we spotted forsythia, plum blossoms, violets, magnolias, shoots for iris, willow trees already in leaf, and other shrubs and trees we weren't familiar with. In the ponds, Seki and I also spotted tadpoles and goldfish. Two men, crouched by the edge of the pond, were scooping out something that turned out to be snails. The other signs of life included couples entwined in each other's arms. As Seki said, "Many lovers here."

As I noted in a previous year, there is a real movement in China to plant trees. As the desert encroaches on farm land and cities—most notably Beijing—the country is trying to hold it back by planting trees and other vegetation. The trees also offset carbon dioxide. China doesn't do things by half measures. In the days of Mao, he offered rewards for the killing of sparrows because the birds helped themselves to wheat and rice crops. The campaign practically eliminated the sparrows, but insects flourished and nearly destroyed the harvest. Sparrows were then permitted to live and multiply.

The new campaign is to plant trees. Here, in College Park, each university has streets lined with trees and shrubs. There are plantings around all the buildings and even groves of trees. Of course, at this moment, the additional disturbance of the earth also increases the dust.

Although Wujin is the newest development area in Changzhou, it is also one of the oldest. A new museum in the area houses artifacts from nearly six thousand years ago. The earliest settlements of Changzhou seem to have originated here. The museum itself and the surrounding buildings (most likely places to eat and sell tourist curios) have been built in the traditional style: curved roofs, white walls, and brown windows.

I believe if I were to return here in another year or two, the area would also have developed more restaurants and shopping centers. Right now, however, it's a bus ride to get groceries and really great dinners.

SEX AND THE SINGLE GIRL

I was amused to see that CNN has finally caught up with the sexual revolution occurring on Chinese university campuses. There has been a steady progression of student coupling since 2000 when I first came to the university here in Changzhou, and this college lagged behind student sexual activity in the major universities in Beijing and Shanghai.

When I first came here, it was rare to see boys and girls walking together. The one day I spotted a boy and girl holding hands, they broke apart and dropped hands when they saw me. More typical was the sight of groups of girls walking together or bands of boys also walking together. The sight of boys holding hands or with arms around each other always made me think how American men would react to this, particularly as some of the boys were in uniform. By the end of the school year, there were a few boy-girl couples; the young foreign teachers who were at the school with me said things were not so innocent as they appeared.

When I returned to the college in 2002, I was struck by how many couples there were so early in the semester. Out for a walk on campus, I often saw couples embracing and kissing. Students had also found a way around strict dormitory supervision, although I imagined it would be hard to conduct any intimacy in dorms that housed a minimum of four girls to a room and eight boys to a room—not to mention attendants on duty in all housing. To maintain a relationship, either one of a couple would rent an apartment, and the other half would "visit." I knew two couples who had such an arrangement. Their garret apartment would have made a perfect setting for *La Bohème*; they said having the place made studying easier and food cheaper. I did not challenge their statement.

On a visit in 2005, I learned student sex life had indeed improved. Condoms were available on campus. Apartments were no longer available for rent, as landlords found it more profitable to rent on a nightly basis. Despite the increase in relationships, the drawbacks to them still keep many girls from beginning one. There are several reasons.

First, of course, is an unwanted pregnancy. In earlier times, a single pregnant woman would have had a difficult time obtaining an abortion. Abortions were available only to married women. Illegal abortions were dangerous, and even those who managed to obtain a legal one were treated miserably by the hospital staff. Today, a pregnant girl will go to a hospital in a large city, and little is said about this. One thing CNN noticed was that the abortion rate for single girls has increased dramatically.

Second, even for a couple devoted to each other, the reality is that their life after graduation will depend on their city of origin and jobs they get. Separation is inevitable.

Third, a sexually experienced woman can have a difficult time finding a husband. Virginity is still prized by many men, and this attitude may take a long time to change.

Presently there are no health centers in universities that offer sex education, as there are in American universities. The *New York Times* has noted an increase in both AIDS and syphilis; most students aren't aware of the dangers of sexually transmitted diseases. Boys are said to avoid using condoms because buying condoms is regarded as shameful. Girls are not educated on the sexually transmitted diseases that may affect pregnancies in the future. So, health care has not caught up with reality here, and many young lives will be damaged as a result.

CHINESE LESSONS AND THE ACCURSED TONES

I am up to my ears in tones. I have Chinese lessons on Friday mornings, and this week's lesson was devoted to practicing tones. Just like singing, one of my Chinese friends said; I didn't have the heart to tell her my singing was also very flat. Still, I believe I am getting the hang of it, and my students love my pronunciation of "sha ke" (fourth tone, for you who know them), as it means "class dismissed." I can also say "shang ke" (fourth tone again), which means "class begins."

Along with our lesson in tones, we were given characters for different foods and how they are prepared. So, today, I went over to the food court to finally read the restaurant menus. I ordered beef with noodles, which turned out to be a bit of a disappointment. The beef was akin to the dried beef often used in chipped-beef dishes at home and was well-hidden under the mounds of noodles. Noodles are generally a North China dish, as wheat is grown in the northern provinces. Rice, however, is grown mainly in the southern provinces and is favored here. However, as times have brought more interactions among the various areas of China, noodles have found a home here. One of Mao's agricultural experiments was to initiate rice cultivation in the north. Thousands of young people were sent to various areas in the north to plant rice. Anchee Min, author of *Red Azalea*, has told her story of working on one of these farms. The experiment was a failure, as were several others of Mao's economic experiments.

But back to my lunch, also a failure of sorts. My "where's the beef?" dish cost me about seventy-five cents. There were a lot of noodles, however, and I decided that seventy-five cents at home wouldn't buy me a plate of spaghetti, so perhaps this wasn't so bad after all.

I have had another adventure with a cell phone purchase. Calling from the telephone in my room is more difficult than sudoku, so I decided to invest in a cell phone. I bought one that cost about fifty dollars. I had to provide my passport to register and then pay about fifteen dollars for a phone card. Apart from the lengthy time, the process went smoothly. Also, the other foreign teacher and I were beneficiaries of a "promotion." These, I believe, change from month to month. We received giant bottles of corn oil; you can figure its tie-in with electronics. I don't get it.

Perhaps if the instructions for using the phone were written in English, I could come to love my cell phone. So far, I have been successful in making two calls and receiving two calls. I have also charged my battery several times. The phone alerts the owner by calling and flashing a light. I wondered who was calling me at 3:00 a.m. one evening and what the burst of light could possibly mean—"battery low," said the little window. So was my possibility of going back to sleep. Generally, my life here is much more accommodating.

MORE CHINESE LESSONS

I can now ask the time in Chinese. I can also ask what time the bank is open. Every Friday I have a Chinese class with Christina, one of the office workers. Learning words and sentences in Chinese is only half of the job of learning this language. The more difficult part is recognizing the characters; even tones pale beside that challenge.

When the Chinese ask you the time, they use the word "dian" (third tone, for those who care), which means "dot." The reference is to the dots on a clock face. Chinese is full of those interesting references, and I enjoy puzzling out how words are formed. Many characters still retain their pictogram beginnings; others have had to work around the new words—such as "computer" and "television"—that have been added to the vocabulary. And, just as we would be hard put to know the meaning of every English word, so too are the Chinese unable to master all the characters in their language.

People here do like challenges. They come in the form of competitions, and I witnessed one over a recent weekend. Students in the School for International Education Exchanges, part of the larger college, competed in designs made of domino-sized colored chips. These, like the domino theory of yore, were set up to fall into their design. The designs mostly celebrated either the school's coming thirty-year anniversary or the Olympics. I had several favorites. One was a computer, complete with a mouse, whose screen held the numeral 30. The other design celebrated both the college's anniversary and the School for International Education Exchanges. The design included several plastic ramps, and as the chips fell, they came up one ramp and set off a small car. This rolled down a second ramp and set off the remaining part of the design.

I had happened on this competition by chance and was the only foreign teacher in attendance. As a result, several students requested me to push the chip that would initiate the remaining dominos. I shook. If I failed to do this properly, I would set back Chinese-American relations more than anything this current administration has done. To my relief, everything went off smoothly, with the result that I was asked to set off another design. I also had to take pictures with everyone.

The next day, while I was out walking, a group of students picnicking in one of the college parks asked me to join them. They wanted to talk to a foreign teacher, something many students here have never done. These casual conversations are much easier and more natural than those in the classroom setting. Most Chinese students are very reluctant to talk in a classroom setting, a challenge for all of us who teach oral English. Yet the day I brought my dulcimer to class and played some songs for them, they sang some of their childhood songs—no hesitation, no embarrassment. Still, when it comes to speaking, pulling teeth would be easier.

CHINESE WOMEN WRITERS

Zhang Xin's collection of four novellas is one of a series of works by contemporary Chinese women writers. Her works portray the lives of today's young women seeking their place in this rapidly developing country. In "Invincible Time," the character Qianzi chooses remaining true to herself rather than settling for cheap but short-term success. In "Where Angels Dare to Tread," two friends finally restore a childhood friendship that has been split by competition for the love of a man and for business success. The workplace puts young women at the mercy of predatory bosses; their success when achieved can ruin marriages or relationships.

Zhang Xin casts an unfriendly eye on men and marriage. Here, for example, she writes: "It suddenly dawned on her that all Chinese men, whether they treated women well or not well, down deep in their hearts, had not so much as a hint of respect or compassion for women." In "Speculators," when the heroine decides to apply for a job in sales, the women tell her, "That's a job not even a man would do. How can a woman like you do it?" Others resent her for trying to succeed, and still others say, "Don't you know that saleswomen would have to go to bed with people first if they want to sell their goods?"

For all his cruel mistakes, Mao did wonders for women. Women, he said, hold up half the sky. He forbade arranged marriages that did not have the woman's assent; he forbade foot-binding (already decreasing); and he recruited women into both the army and the workplace, where they were equals in pay and positions. Yet today, many women would recognize the difficulties Chinese women face in this still male-dominated society. Fewer women serve in the national government, and women students will say that even though they have better grades and performance records than male students, the men will get the jobs. As for power positions in business, women students in 2000 were already talking about "glass ceilings."

This situation will be even less likely to change if, as reported in the newspapers, there is a resurgence of interest in studying Confucius. In his work, the scholar-philosopher assigned women the task of serving not only her husband but any of their sons. She has no independent role. She is responsible only for the harmony in the family. This harmony is necessary for the nation. If there is peace in the family, goes the saying, there is peace in the village. If there is peace in the village, there is peace in the town. And if there is peace in the town, there is peace in the country. Harmony is essential to much of Confucius and, since it is akin to "stability," makes studying Confucius a boon to both men and the country. Of course, the price for this will be paid mostly by women.

BEAUTIFUL CHINESE WOMEN AND MARRIAGE

Being beautiful for today's young Chinese woman has been defined by the media, and so a girl is beautiful if she is slim and fair skinned and has long legs and big eyes. Thus, it isn't a surprise to see female college students wearing three-inch heels to make their legs seem longer and carrying umbrellas to protect themselves from the sun's tanning rays. I'm not certain what steps they might take to widen their eyes, but it has been apparent that many women are toying with anorexia to make certain they remain slim. I want to tell them that, no matter what, most of them will find a mate if they so choose. My class of young faculty proved that many times over, and I recall one member of the class saying that her father told her when she was little that since she wasn't pretty, she had to be clever. She was, and she was also married.

The marriage age in China is set by law, and although I've heard that the legal age of twenty for women and twenty-two for men is lower in the countryside, I have not found that to be true in my research. The ages may also be higher depending on the couple's workplace. At the college, for instance, the man had to be twenty-five and the woman twenty-three. The penalty for ignoring the workplace requirement is loss of job. Many young men and women often set up their apartments and live together until they reach the proper age. The ages were set as part of China's desire to limit the population, known as the one-child policy.

The one-child policy also had some variations. For instance, the minorities—there are fifty-six in China—had no limits, and farm families were also permitted to have more than one child, particularly if there were no sons. Another exception was for a first child born with either a physical or mental disability. Divorce also provided a way around the limit. Divorced men who remarried could have a child with their new wife.

Most of my faculty students agreed with the one-child policy, recognizing the need to curtail population growth. At the same time, they expressed fears about the possible loss of an only child and were concerned about spoiling an only child—"little emperors."

Although sons were sill favored, parents of girls wanted to see their daughters succeed just as well as boys.

The attitude toward female children has shifted and most likely will continue to do so.

Most couples will have their child within the first year or two of their marriage. This, one of the class told me, was so their parents were still young enough to care for the child. Grandparents remain the caretakers of their grandchildren.

A NEW FRIEND AND A NEW TEACHING TOOL

I usually took my lunches in the faculty dining room. I found the offerings varied and plentiful. The dining room was also a good place to find friends. It was also the place where I met Li Xiazhang. He asked if he could join me, and my yes was the beginning of a long friendship. Mr. Li was working on his dissertation in physics; he also had excellent English, the result of having spent several years at the University of Delaware doing graduate work. We always had a lot to talk about, although I now remember little of it. We did joke about two subjects: his wish to be like James Bond and the college president being his chauffeur. President Chen lived in the same area of Nanjing as Mr. Li; he drove there most weekends and gave Mr. Li a ride.. Thanks to Mr.

Li, I had a tour of the graduate science labs and later on that semester an invitation to join him in Nanjing to meet his younger brother, a student at the university there. Our conversations frequently extended beyond lunch, when he walked me back to the guesthouse where I lived. Partly, he wanted to avoid going back to writing his dissertation, which, as I remember, had to be done in both Chinese and English. I tried to convince him to use some of the free-writing techniques we writing faculty had used to help students overcome writing blocks but to no avail. The technique was also a hard sell to most Chinese students, and my success in this attempt was middling.

One of the classroom challenges I also faced was finding a way to get every student to speak and to contribute in class. For the tourist class, I set up teams, each team to present a tour of a major world river with the aim of informing the tourists about the country and the major sights they would visit. The assignment worked well, and each member of the team had something to present. In one of my English classes, I assigned half the class Walt Whitman's "Song of Myself" and the other half Allen Ginsburg's "Howl" and asked them to discuss the two very different views of America. In my business-writing class, I introduced the concept of clustering. Here, a word is put on the blackboard, and students are asked to come up with as many associations with the word as possible. The associations can then be grouped, or clustered, around similar associations. From these, students can see the many ways there are to research and then write a paper.

The last idea I came up with was to organize panel discussions. This worked well with the physical setup of the classroom, where each row of five seats was bolted to the floor and each seat bolted to each other. The concept of a panel discussion was new to my students. I explained that each student in a row was to offer a point of view about a questions, and then they were to agree on a joint opinion to present to the class. I then handed out a question to each row in the class. The questions all related to dating and boy/girl relationships. As you may imagine, the discussions were lively and led to some interesting views on sexism.

OFF TO NANJING

Tuesday I went to Nanjing to visit a friend. It turned out to be the Tuesday that the Olympic torch was going through this old capital city of China, and the city, which has a sizable population, was even more crowded than usual. I came away with a heart sticker and a Chinese flag, both of them featuring the gold stars in the red field that is China's national flag. The four small stars stand for workers, students, farmers, and the army; the large star is the combination of the four.

I did not stand and wave my flag, however, as my purpose was to meet with Helen. She is a history teacher now at Nanjing University and a former student in the class of faculty I taught my first time here in China. I am grateful to her for many things. When I used to teach the class, I often read them English translations of Chinese poetry. No one recognized the English version, so Helen researched the titles and came to class with both the English and the Chinese to show to the class. This was great for me as well, because I could hear how rhymes sound in Chinese. Most translations of Chinese poetry go for the meaning rather than the rhyme. Helen also gave me a book of Mao's poetry. I hadn't known then that the Chairman wrote poetry and discovered he was a considerable poet.

Helen taught history at Jiangsu Polytechnic, and one of her courses was on the Cultural Revolution. I was surprised to learn that the course put the blame squarely on Mao, where usually the blame had been placed on his wife, a leader of the Gang of Four. I asked if this information was generally taught and wondered why Mao was now properly credited with the horrors of that period. The answer was "So something like it could never happen again."

The day was also spent revisiting the Nanjing Art Museum and the Museum of the Massacre. This moving story of the rape of Nanjing is now housed in an updated building and with a better display of photographs and artifacts from that time. The old museum was heartbreaking in itself, but the new structure and displays tell the story more effectively. Both the old and new can make one weep.

I also visited Nanjing University, the oldest in China. The buildings and campus are both lovely, and I felt at home here because both reminded me so of American college campuses. There I met Mr Li and was introduced to his younger brother, an English and literature major at the university

On my return home to Changzhou, I received the following email from Helen:

> Dear Pat:
>
> It's really very nice to meet you today, actually it's moving to see you in Nanjing (according to Chinese etiquette, I should pay a visit to you in Changzhou, and sorry for not being able to do that because of my son living here with me). Thank you enormously for your information about my research and for your beautiful calligraphy (better than mine), it's a nice memory.
>
> Attached are some photos of you. I'll send them to you in two emails.
>
> All best wishes!

Actually, it was Helen who helped me. She was additionally a wonderful resource of Chinese history.

FINAL GOODBYE TO CHANGZHOU

Once more I head for home. This year has been my last to teach in China, so it is a double goodbye, to both the city and the country. In many ways, however, both will be with me for the rest of my life. The great gift of living in another country whose culture and history are so radically different from one's own is learning to see the world in an entirely new way.

From childhood, I have been fascinated by a language that used characters instead of letters and that was written with a brush rather than a pen or pencil. Taking calligraphy lessons was one of my joys in China. Eight strokes replaced twenty-six letters, and "writing" them required patience and concentration. This art was a mental tai chi, and practicing left me both calm and refreshed. I also learned respect for my tools. A new paper could absorb ink more rapidly, changing how quickly I needed to work. When a favorite brush wore out, a new one had to be tamed. Inks also varied. Thus, old and new were constants. All of this provided a philosophy of being.

And, then, there were the stories, and I shall leave you with two. Be like a block of wood, advised Lao-tzu, author of the *Tao Te Ching*, or the book of the way. Now, you may ask, what is "the way"? And the answer is that those who can explain it don't understand it and those who know it can't explain it. Perhaps, the story of the butcher can provide some insight. In all his working years, he never had to sharpen his knife. He knew just where his knife could slip in without hitting bone, so his knife never became dull.

Confucius also has a lesson. Riding along one day with one of his students, they heard a woman wailing loudly, and Confucius asked his student to find out what caused her grief. The woman said a man-eating tiger in the country had just eaten her last son. Confucius then told the student to ask her why she didn't move to another place. He came back to say the woman told him a tyrant ruled in the next province. Confucius then said, "It is better to live with a man-eating tiger than to live without freedom."

There is also the continuing pleasure of reading the great Chinese classics—*Journey to the West, The Three Kingdoms, Dream of the Red Chamber*—as well as the great poets. It will never really be a farewell to China.

AFTERWORD

It has been ten years since I was last in China, and I am now halfway through my ninth decade. Pulling together these notes from a period of eight years, two things struck me. The first was the growth of the city where I had taught, which seemed to transform itself with each of my teaching periods. What I see in retrospect was how masterful a job of planning the Chinese government had devised.

As I mentioned several times, Changzhou was an industrial enterprise city, one of a few that Deng Xiaoping had selected in the quest to move China into the global market. He feared what could happen if the change occurred too swiftly. What made Changzhou such an excellent choice was its location. Midway between Shanghai and Nanjing, it was accessible by rail and highways as well as by boat. The Yangzi provided east-to-west transport, and the Grand Canal provided shipping north and south in the interior. Changzhou offered a less expensive place than Shanghai or Nanjing for new business. Those cities also drew tourists.

The planning included making the city a major visitor's site. Thus, the dinosaur park that was just opening in 2000 was destined to be not only an excellent museum but also a theme park, complete with rides and food concessions. The widened highways, the tree-lined streets, and the "pocket" parks that were added made one of my friends say Changzhou was the most beautiful Chinese city she had stayed in.

The last element needed to make Changzhou a major city was College Park. This, too, developed during my several teaching visits. Jiangsu Institute of Petrochemical Technology changed to a polytechnic institute to a university with many added majors as well as a sizable student body of fifteen thousand. The park also had five additional colleges, each with its own campus and unique architecture, making Changzhou a competitive city for attracting students.

Supermarkets abounded and major name-brand stores featured expensive luxury goods from all over the world. And, of course, there were KFC, McDonald's, Pizza Hut, Starbucks, and Walmart. Changzhou was a world-class city but no longer the place I loved.

The second thing to strike me was how today's China was evident as early as my first visit in 2000. However, few people were paying attention. Some of the New Zealanders among the teachers remarked that the coming century would belong to China. During the controversy over the 2000 presidential election in the United States, China television was reporting on Jiang Zemin's trip through South America, forging relationships with that continent's countries, a trip duplicated later in Africa. My Chinese students easily defined what made a great power: good economy, strong military, and advanced technology. The Chinese government recognized this as well and set its sights on gaining primacy on the world stage.

Although there are some bumps in the Chinese economy, it is still strong; the military has both grown and modernized, and technology, too, is more competitive. Today, China is a world power and seems ready to flex its muscles How that country chooses to use that power is uncertain. I had once thought that the United States and China could be effective leaders in meeting the challenges the world faces today. I believe China's emphasis on harmony provides a fine balance to our American individualism. Much will depend on the leadership of each country, which at present doesn't look promising.

CPSIA information can be obtained
at www.ICGtesting.com
Printed in the USA
BVHW092128060819
555246BV00003B/9/P